MULTICULTURAL EDUCATION SERIES

James A. Banks, Series Editor

Multicultural Education, Transformative Knowledge, and Action
James A. Banks, Editor

Educating Citizens in a Multicultural Society
James A. Banks

Educating Citizens in a Multicultural Society

James A. Banks

Teachers College
Columbia University
New York and London

Published by Teachers College Press, 1234 Amsterdam Avenue, New York, NY 10027

The author is grateful to the following organizations and publishers for granting him permission to reprint the following articles and book chapters that he authored:

The National Council for the Social Studies for: Cultural democracy, citizenship education, and the American dream (presidential address). *Social Education, 47*(3), 178-179, 222-232. (1983).

National Society for the Study of Education for: Values, ethnicity, social science research, and educational policy. In B. Ladner (Ed). *The humanities in precollegiate education* (83rd Yearbook of the NSSE; pp. 91-111). Chicago: University of Chicago Press, 1984.

Howard University for: Ethnicity, class, cognitive, and motivational styles: Research and teaching Implications. *The Journal of Negro Education, 57*(4), 452-466. (1988).

Addison Wesley Longman for Figure 14.4 (p. 457) in *Teaching strategies for the social studies: Inquiry, valuing, and decision-making* (with A. A. Clegg, Jr.). New York: Longman, 1990. Copyright © 1990 by Longman Publishers. Reprinted by permission.

Heldref Publications for: Citizenship education in a pluralistic democratic society. *The Social Studies, 81*(5), 210-214. Reprinted with permission of the Helen Dwight Reid Educational Foundation. Published by Heldref Publications, 1319 18th St. NW, Washington, DC 20036-1802. Copyright © 1990.

The University of South Carolina for: Teaching multicultural literacy for teachers. *Teaching Education, 4*(1), 135-144. (1991).

Macmillan Library Reference USA for an excerpted and adapted version of: Multicultural education for young children: Racial and ethnic attitudes and their modification. (1993). In B. Spodek (Ed.), *Handbook of research on the education of young children* (pp. 236-250). New York: Macmillan. Copyright © 1995 by Bernard Spodek. Used by permission of Macmillan Library Reference USA, a Division of Simon & Schuster.

The National Association of Multicultural Education for: Multicultural education as an academic discipline: Developing scholars and scholarship for the 21st century. *Multicultural Education, 1*(2), 8-11, 38. (1993).

Allyn & Bacon for Figure 3.6 (p. 60) from *Multiethnic education: Theory and practice* (3rd ed.). Boston: Allyn & Bacon. Copyright © 1994 by Allyn and Bacon, a Division of Simon & Schuster.

The Ohio State University College of Education for: C. A. M. Banks & J. A. Banks. (1995). Equity pedagogy: An essential component of multicultural education. *Theory into Practice, 34*(3), 152-158. Copyright © 1995 by The Ohio State University.

Howard University for: Multicultural education and curriculum transformation. *The Journal of Negro Education, 64*(4), 390-400. (1995). This article was the 1995 Charles H. Thompson Lecture presented at Howard University, Washington, DC, November 1, 1995.

Prentice-Hall for: Teaching social studies for decision-making and action. In C. A. Grant & M. L. Gomez (Eds.), *Making schooling multicultural: Campus and classroom* (pp. 221-241). Englewood Cliffs, NJ: Merrill/Prentice Hall, 1996. Reprinted by permission of Prentice-Hall, Upper Saddle River, NJ.

Library of Congress Cataloging-in-Publication Data
Banks, James A.
    Educating citizens in a multicultural society / James A. Banks.
       p. cm. — (Multicultural education series)
    Includes bibliographical references and index.
    ISBN 0-8077-3631-7 (pbk. : alk. paper). — ISBN 0-8077-3632-5
(cloth : alk. paper)
      1. Multicultural education—United States.   2. Citizenship—Study
and teaching—United States. I. Title. II. Series: Multicultural
education series (New York, N.Y.)
    LC1099.3.B364   1997
    370.117'0973—dc21   97-3895
ISBN 0-8077-3631-7 (paper)
ISBN 0-8077-3632-5 (cloth)

Printed on acid-free paper

Manufactured in the United States of America

04   03   02   01   8   7   6   5   4   3

CONTENTS

SERIES FOREWORD

The nation's deepening ethnic texture, interracial tension and conflict, and the increasing percentage of students who speak a first language other than English make multicultural education an imperative as we enter a new century. The 1990 Census indicated that one of every four Americans is a person of color. About one out of every three Americans will be a person of color by the turn of the century.

American classrooms are experiencing the largest influx of immigrant students since the turn of the century. More than 8 million legal immigrants settled in the United States between 1981 and 1990 (U.S. Bureau of the Census, 1994). A large but undetermined number of undocumented immigrants also enter the United States each year. The influence of an increasingly ethnically diverse population on the nation's schools, colleges, and universities is and will continue to be enormous. In 50 of the nation's largest urban public school systems, African Americans, Hispanics, Asian Americans, and other students of color made up 76.5% of the student population in 1992 (Council of the Great City Schools, 1994). In some of the nation's largest cities and metropolitan areas, such as Chicago, Los Angeles, Washington, DC, New York, Seattle, and San Francisco, half or more of the public school students are students of color. In California, the percentage of students of color in the public schools has exceeded the percentage of White students since the 1988–89 school year.

Students of color will make up about 46% of the nation's student population by 2020 (Pallas, Natriello, & McDill, 1989). Fourteen percent of school-age youth live in homes in which English is not the first language (U.S. Bureau of the Census, 1994). Most teachers now in the classroom and in teacher education programs are likely to have students from diverse ethnic, cultural, and racial groups in their classrooms during their careers. This is true for both inner-city and suburban teachers.

An important goal of multicultural education is to improve race relations and to help all students acquire the knowledge, attitudes, and skills needed to participate in cross-cultural interactions and in personal, social, and civic action that will help make our nation more democratic and just. Multicultural education is consequently as important for middle-class White suburban students as it is for students of color who live in the inner city. Multicultural education fosters the public good and the overarching goals of the commonwealth.

The major purpose of the *Multicultural Education Series* is to provide preservice educators, practicing educators, graduate students, and scholars with an interrelated and comprehensive set of books that summarize and analyze important research, theory, and practice related to the education of ethnic, racial, cultural, and language groups in the United States and the education of mainstream students about ethnic and cultural diversity. The books in the *Series* provide research, theoretical, and practical knowledge about the behaviors and learning characteristics of students of color, language-minority students, and low-income students. They also provide knowledge about ways to improve race relations in educational settings.

The definition of multicultural education in the *Handbook of Research on Multicultural Education* (Banks & Banks, 1995b) is used in the *Series:* "Multicultural education is a field of study designed to increase educational equity for all students that incorporates, for this purpose, content, concepts, principles, theories, and paradigms from history, the social and behavioral sciences, and particularly from ethnic studies and women studies" (p. xii). In the *Series*, as in the *Handbook*, multicultural education is considered a "metadiscipline."

The dimensions of multicultural education, developed by Banks (1995a) and described in the *Handbook of Research on Multicultural Education*, provide the conceptual framework for the development of the books in the *Series*. They are: *content integration, the knowledge construction process, prejudice reduction, an equity pedagogy*, and *an empowering school culture and social structure*. To implement multicultural education effectively, teachers and administrators must attend to each of the five dimensions of multicultural education. They should use content from diverse groups when teaching concepts and skills, help students to understand how knowledge in the various disciplines is constructed, help students to develop positive intergroup attitudes and behaviors, and modify their teaching strategies so that students from different racial, cultural, and social-class groups will experience equal educational opportunities. The total environment and culture of the school must also be transformed so that students from diverse ethnic and cultural groups will experience equal status in the culture and life of the school.

Although the five dimensions of multicultural education are highly inter-related, each requires deliberate attention and focus. Each book in the series will focus on one or more of the dimensions, although each book will deal with all of them to some extent because of the highly interrelated characteristics of the dimensions. The first book in the Series, *Multicultural Education, Transformative Knowledge, and Action* (Banks, 1996b) focuses on knowledge construction and action but includes several important chapters on prejudice reduction. This second book in the *Series* discusses each of the five dimensions but focuses on knowledge construction, equity pedagogy, and prejudice reduction. Future books in the *Series*, which will be written by authors of diverse academic and ethnic backgrounds, will present myriad perspectives on research, policy, and practice in multicultural education.

James A. Banks
Series Editor

PREFACE

Our nation's motto is *e pluribus unum*—out of many, one. Throughout most of its history, the United States has been able to forge a shared community by imposing on the *pluribus* (the many) the dominant culture constructed by the elite descendants of the British who settled in America. European males from many different lands, by surrendering their primordial cultural characteristics and attaining those of Anglo Americans, were able to become full citizens and participants in the commonwealth.

Becoming citizens of the commonwealth has been much more difficult for ethnic groups of color and for women from all racial, ethnic, and cultural groups than for mainstream males. Groups of color have experienced three major problems in becoming citizens of the United States. First, they were denied legal citizenship by laws. Second, when legal barriers to citizenship were eliminated, they were often denied educational experiences that would enable them to attain the cultural and language characteristics needed to function effectively in the mainstream society. Third, they were often denied the opportunity to fully participate in mainstream society even when they attained these characteristics because of racial discrimination. Consequently, Gordon (1964) describes U.S. society as characterized by high levels of cultural assimilation and structural pluralism. Because of the institutionalized discrimination in America in both the past and present, Americans from all racial and ethnic groups confine many of their activities to their social-class subsociety within their ethnic group, called an ethclass by Gordon.

The democratic ideals set forth in the nation's founding documents (the Declaration of Independence, the Constitution, and the Bill of Rights) and the racial, gender, and class discrimination that is widespread within American society create a serious dilemma in educating students to become reflective, thoughtful, and active citizens. This *citizenship dilemma* has intensified since the Immigration Reform Act of 1965 was enacted. Since this act became effective in 1968, the characteristics of the nation's immigrants have changed substantially. During most of the nation's history, the largest proportion of its immigrants have come from Europe. However, between 1981 and 1986, only 11% of the nation's legal immigrants came from Europe; 85% came from Latin America and Asia (U.S. Bureau of the Census, 1994).

The thousands of immigrants who enter the United States each year from Asia, Latin America, and Europe speak a variety of languages and have many cultural characteristics that are highly inconsistent with those established within our society and within the schools. The 1990 Census indicated that about 14% of the nation's school-age youth (aged 5 to 17) lived in homes where the primary language was not English (U.S. Bureau of the Census, 1994). The Census predicts that nearly half (47.5%) of the nation's citizens will be individuals of color by 2050.

The changing ethnic texture of the United States intensifies the challenge of educating citizens and creating an authentic *unum* that has moral authority. An *authentic unum* reflects the experiences, hopes, and dreams of all the nation's citizens. An *imposed unum*, the kind that has existed throughout most of the nation's history, reflects one dominant cultural group. It does not have moral authority and legitimacy with most of the nation's citizens. An imposed *unum* will be more difficult to maintain in the future than it was in the past because of the renewed quests by marginalized groups for inclusion and equity and because of the nation's changing ethnic characteristics. Our challenge as a new century begins is to establish an authentic *unum* that has moral authority and yet create moral, civic, and just communities in which citizens from diverse racial, ethnic, and cultural communities will participate and to which they will have allegiance.

As we enter a new century, the question of how best to educate citizens to function effectively in a multicultural society will become increasingly important as the ethnic texture of our nation deepens and the social-class schism continues to widen. The renewed quests by groups on the margins of society for full structural inclusion will also intensify the citizenship dilemma in the United States. However, most of the educational literature on citizenship education and creating democratic schools is silent on questions related to race, ethnicity, and social-class stratification. Dealing effectively with these issues is an essential component of a civic education project in a pluralistic democratic state. This book is designed to help fill this gap in the literature.

The concepts, paradigms, and aims of multicultural education must become integral parts of the project to educate citizens and to create democratic schools in a free society. This book consists of ten articles and chapters I wrote during a 13-year period that examine issues, concepts, perspectives, and possibilities for educating citizens in a pluralistic democratic society. Despite strong temptations to the contrary, I have left the papers essentially as they were first published, with the exception of making some of the titles more succinct, correcting obvious errors, and occasionally updating terminology. I have also made all citations consistent with the *Publication Manual of the American Psychological Association*.

This book is divided into four parts. Part I, which includes an introductory essay written especially for this book, describes the challenges and possibilities of educating students for citizenship in a pluralistic democratic society. As a social studies educator who has been deeply concerned about citizenship issues throughout my three-decade career, I helped to construct the field of multicultural education in part because I viewed it as a vehicle to help students and groups on the margins become effective and transformative citizens in the mainstream of the commonwealth.

The ways in which knowledge is constructed by social scientists and the ways in which it influences teachers and students are discussed in Part II. Some knowledge created by social scientists promotes freedom, democracy, and justice and, consequently, supports citizenship education in free societies. Examples are works by Gould (1981), Collins (1990), and Franklin (1993). Other knowledge, such as that contained in *Losing Ground* by Murray (1984) and *The Bell Curve* by Herrnstein and Murray (1994), legitimizes oppression and supports social, economic, and political hegemony. Freedom of speech, a hallmark of democratic societies, permits both oppressive and liberatory knowledge and paradigms to flow without constraints. The challenge to educating democrats is to help them learn the skills—and acquire the will—to uncover and challenge oppressive ideologies and to support those that liberate with personal, social, and civic action.

Part III describes the five dimensions of multicultural education that I discuss extensively in the *Handbook of Research on Multicultural Education* (Banks, 1995a). The dimensions can serve as a helpful guide to educators when they are reforming schools to make them more democratic and to increase their capacity to educate students from diverse groups to become thoughtful and active citizens. The chapters in Part III discuss three of the dimensions in depth: knowledge construction, equity pedagogy, and prejudice reduction.

The most effective way to educate students for participation in a democratic society is for teachers, administrators, and other members of the school staff to model democratic behavior in their interactions with each other and with students. Part IV describes issues related to the effective education of teachers, scholars, and other educational leaders so that they will be able to conceptualize, design, and implement projects and programs that promote citizenship in free societies. The final chapter, which was my National Council for the Social Studies presidential address, is a comprehensive blending of my interest in citizenship education and in multicultural education.

It takes a caring and nurturing village to socialize a child in a tightly segregated community to become someone optimistic about the possibilities of democracy in America. I am deeply indebted to my parents, and to the teachers in the Arkansas community in which I grew up in the 1940s and 1950s, for my commitment to American democratic ideals and for keeping faith in their promise as I undertake my work. My parents, who farmed cotton in a precarious environment frequently plagued by boll weevils and inclement weather, were my first and most important models of committed democrats. No farm duty or task ever kept them from the long journey to town to cast their votes. My teachers, in both words and deeds, exemplified excellence, compassion, and a belief in the possibility to achieve against the odds. That they kept their faith in America and its promise of democracy is a testament to their powerful legacy, which I cherish.

I am grateful to Cherry A. McGee Banks, my colleague and best friend for over a quarter of a century, for her critical and thoughtful reading of my work. She has read every word in this book and has been a source of encouragement and support during the 13-year period in which the essays that make up this book were written. Our children, Angela and Patricia, are active participants in our project to extend democracy in our schools and society.

I wish to thank Karen Gourd, a research assistant in the Center for Multicultural Education, for helping to prepare the manuscript for submission to the publisher. I am grateful to Brian Ellerbeck and Peter Sieger at Teachers College Press for the care, expertise, and speed with which the manuscript was reviewed, produced, and published.

Educating
Citizens
in a
Multicultural
Society

PART I

Citizenship Education and Diversity

A fundamental premise of a democratic society is that citizens will participate in the governing of the nation and that the nation-state will reflect the hopes, dreams, and possibilities of its people. People are not born democrats. Consequently, an important goal of the schools in a democratic society is to help students acquire the knowledge, values, and skills needed to participate effectively in public communities.

Educating students to be democrats is a challenge in any kind of society (Parker, 1996). It is a serious challenge in a society characterized by cultural, ethnic, racial, and language diversity, especially when these variables are used to privilege individuals from some groups and to deny others equal opportunities to participate. Educating students for effective citizenship has been a problem in the United States since the nation's beginning because of the way in which the Founding Fathers defined "We the people" in the Constitution. "We the people" referred to White males who were property owners. African Americans, Native Americans, women from all racial and ethnic groups, and White males without property were denied the privileges of citizenship in the commonwealth.

Although the Founding Fathers constructed a limited and particularistic conception of citizenship at the nation's beginning, the longevity and power of the Constitution has been due to its elasticity. The Constitution's elasticity (e.g., the possibility for amendments) has enabled it to be expanded so that people of color and women have attained expanded rights through the centuries.

Citizenship education should also help all students, including mainstream students, to acquire the knowledge, values, and skills needed to interact positively with people from diverse ethnic, racial, and cultural groups and to develop a commitment to act to make their communities, the nation, and the world moral, civic, and equitable.

The quests for freedom by people of color are continuing, and their dreams in America are still deferred. Consequently, essential goals of citizenship education in the United States are to help students of color to attain the knowledge, values, and skills needed to participate effectively in mainstream civic and work communities as well as to participate in civic action that will help to transform our nation in ways that will make it more just and humane.

This part of the book examines issues related to citizenship in pluralistic democratic societies.

1

RECONSTRUCTING CITIZENSHIP EDUCATION

Whenever I think about the meaning of citizenship education in a multicultural society, memories of being an elementary school child in a racially segregated school in the South in the 1940s and 1950s surface. Each morning, we said the Pledge of Allegiance and sang both the national anthem and the "Negro" national anthem, "Lift Every Voice and Sing." Saying that we lived in a nation "with liberty and justice for all" within a segregated school symbolized the challenge of educating citizens in a society stratified by race and class. A stated goal of the social studies program in the Lee County (Arkansas) Public Schools was to develop good citizens. By requiring us to sing both the national and the Negro national anthems, our teachers were trying to help us develop respect for our ethnic heritage as well as loyalty to the nation-state and its symbols.

My early school experiences, Frederick Douglass's Fourth of July speech in 1852, "What to the Slave Is the Fourth of July?" (Frederick Douglass Discusses, 1968), the forced removal of the Cherokee from their homeland in 1838–39, the internment of Japanese Americans during World War II, and the increasing racial and class segregation in the nation's schools epitomize the dilemma of educating citizens in a diverse society stratified by race and class. These events evoke these questions about citizenship education in a culturally and ethnically diverse society:

- What is the meaning and latent function of citizenship education in a society highly stratified by race, class, and gender?
- Is it possible for citizenship education to promote justice in a highly stratified society or does citizenship education necessarily reflect and reproduce the society in which it is embedded?
- Whose concept is *citizenship education*? To whom does the concept belong? Who constructed it? Whose interests does it serve? Whose lived experiences does it reflect? Can individuals and groups on the margins of society effectively participate in a transformation of the concept and of society?

3

Citizenship education has been constructed historically by powerful and mainstream groups and has usually served their interests. It has often fostered citizen passivity rather than action, taught students large doses of historical myths in its attempts to develop patriotism, conceptualized citizenship responsibility primarily as voting, and reinforced the dominant social, racial, and class inequality in American society. In other words, citizenship education in the United States has historically reinforced dominant-group hegemony and student inaction. Writes Baldwin (1985):

> The purpose of education . . . is to create in a person the ability to look at the world for himself, to make his own decisions, to say to himself this is black or this is white, to decide for himself whether there is a God in heaven or not. To ask questions of the universe, and then to live with those questions, is the way he achieves his identity. But no society is really anxious to have that kind of person around. What society really, ideally, wants is a citizenry that will simply obey the rules of society. If a society succeeds in this, that society is about to perish. (p. 326)

As we approach a new century, it is essential that educators explore the possibility of transforming citizenship education so that it will deal with struggle, tension, conflict, and the need to construct an authentic *unum*, not one imposed on those who are victimized and marginalized. Citizenship education must also help in the construction of a transformed national identity that reflects the hopes, dreams, and realities of all of the nation's citizens and to which they can and will be loyal and patriotic. The aim of citizenship education should be to attain a delicate balance between education for unity and nationhood and educating citizens to recognize, confront, and help resolve inequality manifested in forms such as racism, sexism, and classism.

THE NATION'S DEEPENING CITIZENSHIP DILEMMA

The historian John Hope Franklin (1995) argues that we inherited our citizenship dilemma from the hallowed men who constructed the Constitution because of the limited way in which "We the people" was defined in the Constitution. The nation's citizenship dilemma is deepening as the gap between the rich and the poor widens, as more and more immigrants from Asia and Latin America rush to this land in search of their dreams, as conservative attacks on the poor become more strident and mean-spirited (M. B. Katz, 1989), and as the nation becomes increasingly characterized by what Gould (1994) calls an era of "unprecedented ungenerosity."

The nation's changing ethnic texture is an important source of the nation's citizenship dilemma and tensions. The nation's population of people of color is considerably outpacing the growth of the White population. However, as the nation's people of color grow in number, so do their poverty and powerlessness. Political and economic power remains highly concentrated among elite White groups, although an important development in the past two decades has been the significant number of people of color—such as African Americans and Latinos—who have entered the middle class. Their social-class mobility has deepened class schism within minority communities. Although the significance of race has not declined in America, as the sociologist William Julius Wilson (1978) implied by the title of his controversial book, he was on the mark when he pointed out that the significance of class has substantially increased in American society since the late 1960s.

As a new century approaches, the challenge of educating citizens from diverse groups who can help construct civic, just, and moral communities that promote the common good is vexing. The need for the schools to play an important role in a civic education project that recognizes both the challenges and opportunities of ethnic, racial, and cultural diversity has perhaps never been greater in the nation's history.

CITIZENSHIP EDUCATION AND THE CONSTRUCTION OF AN AUTHENTIC UNUM

The motto of the United States is *e pluribus unum*—out of many, one. Important and essential questions within a democratic society are:

Who participates in constructing the *unum*?
To whom does the *unum* belong?
Whom does it benefit?
Who defines its boundaries?
Who decides who can participate in its construction and reconstruction?
Who decides when it will be constructed and reconstructed?
How can the *unum* be reconstructed when many groups within the *pluribus* feel alienated by the *unum* and its goals and symbols? In other words, when we state that our nation's motto is *e pluribus unum*, we need to ask, "Whose *unum*?"

An *unum* is authentic and legitimate within a democratic, pluralistic society only when the diverse racial, ethnic, cultural, social-class, and gender groups within the nation-state are participating fully in its construction and reconstruction and are helping to determine its aims, goals, and values. These groups must also perceive the *unum* as consistent with their struggles, hopes, dreams, and possibilities. They also must experience—or believe that they can experience—equal status within the nation-state and believe that the nation-state and its symbols and interests reflect their values, perspectives, and goals.

The *Unum* and the Constitution

A *unum* that does not have the characteristics described above is not authentic. It is an imposed *unum*. The Constitution of the United States, when first formulated by the Founding Fathers, defined "We the people" as Anglo-Saxon males with property (Franklin, 1989, 1995). This conception of the *unum* was restrictive and particularistic. However, the genius of the Constitution is that it also conceptualized and legitimized democratic ideals, such as liberty, justice, and equality, that could, through a process of action by citizens, be expanded to include women, people of color, and working-class people.

The Constitution consequently provides an excellent and powerful framework for creating a pluralistic society in which democratic citizenship becomes possible (Kymlica, 1995). Democratic citizenship is possible in a society when diverse groups can participate in action that will deepen and extend human rights and justice in a nation-state. The civil rights movement, the women's rights movement, and the movement for the rights of people with disabilities used the Constitution to legitimize their quests for human rights and inclusion.

Martin Luther King, Jr., Fannie Lou Hamer, Ella Baker, and the other leaders of the civil rights movement used the ideals in the nation's founding documents as a major source for the aims and goals of a project designed to rid the nation of racial segregation and inequality. These leaders were able to use the values of the American Creed described in the Declaration of Independence, the Constitution, and the Bill of Rights as a rationale to extend rights to people and groups on the margins of society.

To become democratic institutions and to contribute to the democratization of society, schools must help students to acquire the knowledge, values, and skills needed to participate in citizen action that will help to actualize for all the ideals that the Founding Fathers intended for an elite few. This is a very important mission of schools in a democratic society.

To prepare effective citizens for living in a democratic society, schools themselves must become democratic institutions that model caring, ethnic diversity, and effective citizen action. Experience speaks much louder than words. In *Experience and Education* John Dewey (1938) points out that students learn most effectively from experience.

A study by Trager and Yarrow (1952) indicates that students who experience a democratic curriculum are more likely to develop democratic attitudes and values than students who experience a nondemocratic curriculum. They studied the effects of a democratic and nondemocratic curriculum on the racial attitudes of first- and second-grade students. The curriculum interventions in this study consisted of reading materials, activities, and teachers who role-played democratic and nondemocratic teaching styles.

After the interventions, the students who participated in the democratic interventions expressed more democratic racial attitudes and behaviors than the students who participated in the interventions that taught the prevailing views and attitudes of U.S. society. The teachers also expressed more positive racial attitudes after the interventions. The authors concluded that students "learn what they live," which is the title of their book-length study.

Expanding the *Unum*

The democratic ideals set forth in the Declaration of Independence and the Constitution were restrictive and particularistic. However, the elasticity of the ideals within these documents—such as justice, equality, and human rights—has enabled them to be expanded since the late eighteenth century to include a range of groups previously excluded and groups on the margins.

The two centuries since the ratification of the Constitution have witnessed tremendous expansion of the ideas formulated by the Founding Fathers to include previously excluded groups. The Constitution has been able to survive in large part because it has within it the possibility for expansion to include more and more segments of "We the people." Yet the expansion to include diverse groups during the last two centuries has not been a linear or steady process. Rather, the nation's history has been characterized by both the expansion and retrenchment of human rights during periods that Arthur M. Schlesinger, Jr. (1986) calls the "cycles of American history."

Many events during the last two centuries created more rights for excluded and marginalized groups, thus making the nation's *unum* more inclusive and authentic. The Bill of Rights, the abolition of slavery, the Thirteenth, Fourteenth, and Fifteenth Amendments to the Constitution, the 1928 Voting Rights Act for Women, the *Brown v. Board of Education* Supreme Court decision of 1954, the Civil Rights Act of 1964, and the Immigration Reform Act of 1965 were landmarks in the nation's quest for justice and equality and in the construction of a just and authentic *unum*.

The quest for human rights and democracy in American society has been slowed, sometimes severely, by antidemocratic movements, ideas, policies, and ideologies. The removal of Native Americans to Indian Territory during the 1830s, the *Plessy v. Ferguson* Supreme Court decision in 1896 that legalized and legitimized racial segregation, the Chinese Exclusion Act of 1882, Executive Order 9066 authorizing the internment of Japanese Americans in 1942, and the nativist movement that tried to close the nation's shores to southern, eastern, and central European immigrants near the turn of the century are powerful examples of historical developments that have severely challenged democracy and freedom in the United States.

THE UNITED STATES TODAY

American society is still characterized by democratic and antidemocratic actions, movements, ideologies, and leaders. Myrdal (1944) called the democratic ideals and antidemocratic practices in American society, such as racial discrimination, an "American dilemma." Myrdal viewed this dilemma as providing possibilities for change and transformation. He argued that most Americans had internalized what he called American Creed values (e.g., justice, equality, and liberty). Consequently, he believed that their internalization of democratic values could become an important factor in motivating them to act to close the gap between their behavior and democratic ideals.

Despite the wide gap between American democratic ideals and practices such as discrimination in U.S. society, the school curriculum, according to researchers such as Sleeter and Grant (1991) and Anyon (1980), often presents a distorted and misleading view of the United States, describing it as a nation that actualizes democracy and that has few problems related to race, gender, or social class. This view of the United States, which historian Joyce Appleby (1992) calls "American exceptionalism," suggests to students that democracy has been attained in the United States and that our racial and gender problems were solved by the civil rights movement of the 1960s and 1970s. The popular culture also reinforces American exceptionalism.

American exceptionalism has often been exemplified in the behavior of U.S. presidents and other political leaders. At the end of the Spanish–American War in 1898, Spain accepted defeat and agreed to give Cuba its independence. At the same time, Spain agreed to give Puerto Rico, another Spanish territory, to the United States. The future of the Philippines was to be decided at a peace meeting.

The peace talks went smoothly until Spain asked to keep the Philippines, which President McKinley demanded that the United States be given. He told a church group about his decision:

> I walked the floor of the White House night after night until midnight. I am not ashamed to tell you gentlemen, that I went down on my knees and prayed to Almighty God for the light and guidance more than one night. And one night late it came to me . . . that there was nothing left for us to do but take them all, and to educate the Filipinos, and uplift and civilize and Christianize them. The next morning I sent for our map-maker. I told him to put the Philippines on the map of the United States. There they are and there they will stay while I am president! (cited in Banks with Sebesta, 1982, p. 122).

On February 4, 1899, the Filipinos revolted against the United States. The United States spent more money and more Americans lost their lives in that war than in the Spanish–American War.

TEACHING ABOUT AMERICAN IDEALS
AND AMERICAN REALITIES

In a democratic curriculum, students need to be taught about and have opportunities to acquire American democratic values while at the same time learning about American realities that challenge these ideals, such as discrimination based on race, gender, and social class. If we essentialize American society in the curriculum by emphasizing ways in which American history has actualized American democratic ideals—as we have often done in the past—students are likely to conclude that we have already attained these ideals and that, consequently, little work is needed to maintain a just and democratic society. If we tell the story of America only as a series of oppressions and exploitations of one group by another, we will distort history and run the risk of making students disillusioned, cynical, and hopeless.

A focus on exploitation is also likely to give students the impression that people of color have only been victims and have not been effective actors, leaders, and shapers of their own history. We need to conceptualize history and the civic education curriculum in ways that will enable students to acquire a comprehensive view of people of color and their interactions with mainstream groups. This comprehensive view would describe people of color as institutional builders who had efficacy and who were shapers of their own destinies. They would not be described only as victims. Reality dictates that we describe slavery, discrimination, the internment of Japanese Americans, and the Trail of Tears. However, ethnic groups of color such as African Americans, Native Americans, and Mexican Americans also shaped their own destinies and built institutions such as schools, churches, businesses, and fraternities. Anglo Americans and people of color who have worked to make our society more just should also be highly visible in the curriculum.

In the democratic curriculum, we must describe the democratic ideals that help to cement our nation, the progress we have made and are making in achieving the ideals, and the important ways in which we have failed—and are failing—as a nation to live up to the ideals. Students can become thoughtful, committed, and effective citizens only when they have internalized democratic ideals, are knowledgeable about the gap between the nation's ideals and its realities, and have the commitment and skills to act to help close that gap.

2

CITIZENSHIP EDUCATION IN A MULTICULTURAL SOCIETY

Mixing and blending citizenship and multicultural education presents tremendous challenges as well as opportunities as the United States enters the twenty-first century. It is easier to describe the challenges that diversity poses to citizenship and citizenship education than to conceptualize, develop, and implement creative ways to deal with these challenges and transform them into opportunities.

A major challenge facing the United States today is how to create effective and reflective citizens out of the thousands of immigrants who are entering the nation each year (Banks, 1991b), and how to structurally include the millions of indigenous people of color who remain largely on the fringes of American society, politically alienated within the commonwealth, and who share little in the nation's wealth. The American dream remains, for most people of color in the United States (e.g., African Americans and Hispanic Americans), elusive and deferred. The gap between the relatively affluent 85% of U.S. society and the desperately poor 15% of the population continues to widen ("An American Vision," 1990). This divide is heavily defined along racial lines.

POVERTY: A CHALLENGE TO CITIZENSHIP EDUCATION

An increasing percentage of the nation's school-age youths are victims of poverty as well as confined and isolated in low-income inner-city communities. In 1990, about one of every four children in the United States was a victim of poverty ("Poverty Rate," 1990). The proportion of children living in poverty is expected to increase in the years ahead, from about 21% of all children in 1984 to 27% of all children in 2020 (Pallas, Natriello, & McDill, 1989). The large number of American youths who are victims of poverty poses a serious problem for the development of effective citizens. Youths who are victims of poverty are at a high risk of becoming school dropouts, experiencing academic failure, and engaging in antisocial behavior.

It is very difficult for youths who drop out of school or who experience academic failure to become effective and productive citizens in a post-industrial knowledge society. Effective citizens in the twenty-first century must have the knowledge, attitudes, and skills needed to compete in a global world economy that is primarily service- and knowledge-oriented. All of the new jobs and most of the new wealth created between now and the turn of the century will be in service industries (Johnston & Packer, 1987). Knowledge-oriented service jobs, in fields such as education, health, and trade, require high-level reasoning, analytical, quantitative, and communication skills. Yet if the current levels of educational attainment among most U.S. youths of color continue, the nation will be hard-pressed to meet its labor needs with its own citizens. There will be a mismatch between the skills of a large percentage of the workers in the United States and the needs of the labor force.

There will not be a sufficient number of Whites, and particularly White males, to meet U.S. labor demands in the early years of the next century. Between 1980 and 2000, about 83% of the new entrants to the labor force will be either women, people of color, or immigrants (Johnston & Packer, 1987). Native White males will make up only 15% of the new entrants to the labor force during this period. Consequently, to meet workforce demands in the early years of the next century, women and people of color will have to enter scientific and technical fields in greater numbers.

CITIZENSHIP EDUCATION FOR A CHANGING AMERICA

An important implication of the demographic trends described above is that a major goal of citizenship education must be to help low-income students and students of color to develop the knowledge, attitudes, and skills needed to participate in the mainstream workforce and in the mainstream society in the twenty-first century. This goal is essential but not sufficient. Nor is it possible to attain without transforming and restructuring institutions and institutionalizing new goals and ideals within them. We must also rethink and transform the goals of our nation-state if we are to enter the twenty-first century as a strong, democratic, and just society.

I do not believe that our schools, as they are currently structured, conceptualized, and organized, will be able to help most students of color, especially those who poor and from cultures that differ from the school culture in significant ways, to acquire the knowledge, attitudes, and skills needed to function effectively in the knowledge society of the next century. Our schools were designed for a different population at a time when immigrant and poor youths did not need to be literate or to have basic skills to get jobs and to become self-supporting citizens.

When large waves of immigrants entered the United States near the turn of the century, jobs in heavy industry requiring little knowledge or skills were available. Thus the school was less important as a job preparatory institution than it is today. Schools have worked best in reinforcing dominant societal ideologies and social-class stratification, as well as helping to socialize youths from various social-class groups into their future societal roles. Our schools have not been required before in our history to perform a transformative function.

To help students of color and low-income students to experience academic success, and thus to become effective citizens, the school must be restructured so that these students will have successful experiences within a nurturing, personalized, and caring environment. Some fundamental reforms will have to occur in schools for this kind of environment to be created. Grouping practices that relegate a disproportionate number of low-income students and students of color to lower-tracked classes in which they receive an inferior education will have to be dismantled (Oakes, 1985). A norm will have to be institutionalized within the schools that states that all students can and will learn, regardless of their home situations, race, social class, or ethnic group.

The theories and interventions developed and implemented by researchers such as Edmonds (1986) and Comer (1988) can help schools bring about the structural changes needed to institutionalize the idea that all children can and will learn. Innovative ways will need to be devised that will involve a joint parent–school effort in the education of students of color. Most parents want their children to experience success in school, even though they may have neither the knowledge nor the resources to actualize their aspirations for their children. Successful educational interventions with low-income students and students of color are more likely to succeed if they have a parent-involvement component, as Comer (1988) has demonstrated with his successful interventions in inner-city, predominantly African American schools. Because of the tremendous changes that have occurred in American families in the last two decades, we need to rethink and reconceptualize what parent involvement means and to formulate new ways to involve parents at a time when large numbers of school-age youths are from single-parent or two–working-parent families.

THE NEED TO CREATE A TRANSFORMED SOCIETY

Our goal should not be merely to educate students of color or White mainstream students to fit into the existing workforce, social structure, and society. Such an education would be inimical to students from different cultural groups because it would force them to experience self-alienation. It would fail to incorporate their voices, experiences, and perspectives. This kind of unidimensional, assimilationist education would also create problems for the citizenship and national identity of youths of color. By forcing them to experience an education, sponsored by the state, that does not reflect their cultures and experiences, the message would be sent that they are not an integral part of the nation-state and national culture. To develop a clarified national identity and commitment to the nation-state, groups and individuals must feel that they are integral parts of the nation-state and national culture.

Citizenship education in a multicultural society must have as an important goal helping all students, including White mainstream students, to develop the knowledge, attitudes, and skills needed to participate within but also to help transform and reconstruct society. Problems such as racism, sexism, poverty, and inequality are widespread in U.S. society and permeate many of the nation's institutions, such as the workforce, the courts, and the schools. To educate future citizens merely to fit into and not to transform society would result in the perpetuation and escalation of these problems, including the widening gap between the rich and the poor, racial conflict and tension, and the growing number of people who are victims of poverty and homelessness.

A society that has sharp divisions between the rich and the poor, and between Whites and people of color, is not a stable one. It contains stresses and tensions that can lead to societal upheavals and racial polarization and conflict. Thus citizenship education for the twenty-first century must not only help students to become literate and reflective citizens who can participate productively in the workforce; it must also teach them to care about other people in their communities and to take personal, social, and civic action to create a humane and just society.

A CURRICULUM FOR MULTICULTURAL LITERACY AND CITIZENSHIP

Students must develop multicultural literacy and cross-cultural competency if they are to become knowledgeable, reflective, and caring citizens in the twenty-first century. To acquire the skills needed for effective citizenship in a multicultural society, students must be helped to view U.S. history and culture from new and different perspectives, must acquire new knowledge about U.S. society, and must be helped to understand knowledge as a social construction. Knowledge is neither neutral nor static; it is culturally based, perspectivistic, dynamic, and changing.

Conceptualizing knowledge as socially constructed and dynamic conflicts with the view of knowledge popularized by writers such as Hirsch (1987) and Ravitch and Finn (1987). These writers conceptualize knowledge as static and neutral and believe that a major goal of schooling should be to help students to memorize lists of facts that have been identified by experts. While it is important for all U.S. citizens to master a common body of knowledge, it is just as important for students to understand the process by which knowledge is created, its latent assumptions and premises, the purposes for which it was created, and the major interests that it serves.

Much of the knowledge institutionalized in the nation's shared institutions, such as schools, colleges, and universities, reflects the interests, goals, and purposes of dominant groups within society. Their interests are described as identical with the public interest. The knowledge institutionalized within the nation's shared institutions should reflect the experiences and goals of all groups within society and should promote justice, the common good, civic virtue, and other democratic values. All groups within society should participate in the construction of this knowledge.

Since the founding of the United States, much of the knowledge that has become institutionalized in educational institutions has perpetuated racism (Franklin, 1976; Ladner, 1973), sexism (Collins, 1990), and inequality (Ryan, 1971). Important examples of such knowledge are the views of slaves as happy and carefree, Indians as hostile, and the idea that the westward expansion of the United States civilized and brought salvation to the American Indians.

Scholars of color have challenged institutionalized views of their people since at least the late nineteenth century, when George Washington Williams published the first history of African Americans in the United States, *History of the Negro Race in America from 1619 to 1880* [2 volumes, 1882, 1883] (Franklin, 1985). Other challenges to institutionalized views of African Americans and other peoples of color were written by scholars such as Carter G. Woodson (1933) and W. E. B. Du Bois (1935/1962), as well as a score of African American, Hispanic, and American Indian scholars in the 1960s and 1970s (Acuña, 1972; Deloria, 1969; Ladner, 1973).

Many of the long-established, blatant stereotypic conceptions of people of color that were institutionalized in educational institutions and in the popular culture have disappeared since they were challenged by the ethnic protest movements of the 1960s and 1970s. However, new and more subtle ones continue to be formulated, popularized, and perpetuated. The "disadvantaged" low-income child of the 1960s has become the "at-risk" child in the 1990s (Cuban, 1989).

To become effective citizens in the twenty-first century, students must be knowledgeable about the conceptions of various ethnic and racial groups within society, how these conceptions were constructed, and their basic assumptions and purposes. They must also be helped to formulate their own knowledge and perceptions of various groups and their roles in society, as well as to develop the ability to rationally justify the validity and accuracy of the knowledge and conceptions they create. Students must become active constructors of as well as thoughtful consumers of social, historical, and political knowledge.

TEACHING ABOUT KNOWLEDGE AS A CONSTRUCTION PROCESS

Teachers can use two important concepts in U.S. history to help students to better understand the ways in which knowledge is constructed and to participate in rethinking, reconceptualizing, and constructing knowledge. *The New World* and *the European discovery of America* are two central ideas that are pervasive in school and university curricula as well as in the popular culture. The teacher can begin a unit focused on these concepts with readings, discussions, and visual presentations that describe the archaeological theories about the peopling of the Americas nearly 40,000 years ago by groups who crossed the Bering Strait while hunting for animals and plants to eat. The students can then study the Aztecs and other highly developed civilizations that developed in the Americas prior to the arrival of the Europeans in the fifteenth century.

After the study of the Native American cultures and civilizations, the teacher can provide the students with brief accounts of some of the earliest Europeans, such as Columbus and Cortés, who came to America. The teacher can then ask the students what they think the term *the New World* means, whose point of view it reflects, and to list other, more neutral words to describe the Americas. The students could then be asked to describe *the European discovery of America* from two different perspectives: (1) that of an Arawak Indian (Olsen, 1974) (the Arawaks were living in the Caribbean when Columbus arrived there in 1492) and (2) that of an "objective" or neutral historian who has no particular attachment to either American Indian or European society.

The major objective of this lesson is to help students to understand knowledge as a social construction and to understand how concepts such as *the New World* and *the European discovery of America* not only are ethnocentric and Eurocentric terms but also are normative concepts that serve latent but important political purposes, that is, to justify the destruction of Native American peoples and civilizations by Europeans such as Columbus and those who came after him. *The New World* is a concept that subtly denies the political existence of the Indians and their nations prior to the coming of the Europeans.

The goal of teaching knowledge as a social construction is not to make students into cynics or to encourage them to desecrate European heroes such as Columbus and Cortés. Rather, the aim is to help students to understand the nature of knowledge, the complexity of the development of U.S. society, as well as to understand how the history that becomes institutionalized in a society primarily reflects the perspectives and points of views of the victors rather than the vanquished. When viewed in a global context, the students will be able to understand how the creation of historical knowledge in the United States parallels the creation of knowledge in other democratic societies and is a much more open and democratic process than in totalitarian nation-states.

Another important goal of teaching knowledge as a construction process is to help students to develop higher-level thinking skills and empathy for the peoples who have been victimized by the expansion and growth of the United States. When diverse and conflicting perspectives are juxtaposed, students are required to compare, contrast, weigh evidence, and make reflective decisions. They are also able to develop an empathy and an understanding of each group's perspective and point of view. The creation of their own versions of events and situations, and new concepts and terms, also requires students to reason at high levels and to think critically about data and information.

TEACHING ABOUT CONTRADICTIONS AND THE FUTURE OF AMERICA

Citizenship education for the twenty-first century must also help students to understand and to deal reflectively with the contradictions that result from the ideals within American society (such as those that make up the American Creed—i.e., liberty, justice, and equality) and the racial discrimination that they will experience and/or observe in history, current affairs, the wider society, or the school community. Too often educators remain silent about these contradictions, thus causing students to become cynical and distrustful of the school and its curriculum. When the school fails to recognize, validate, and testify to the racism, poverty, and inequality that students experience in their daily lives, they are likely to view the school and the curriculum as contrived and sugar-coated constructs that are out of touch with the real world and the struggles of their daily lives.

The school must confront and help students to deal reflectively with what Myrdal (1944) called "the American dilemma," the situation created by the gap between American democratic ideals and American racism. Some people of color, both children and adults, feel a modicum of resentment and betrayal when they are required to say these words in the Pledge of Allegiance: "With liberty and justice for all." The school should recognize that such ambivalent feelings are caused by the institutionalized racism and discrimination that people of color have experienced historically and still experience today.

The school should also help students to recognize and understand the ambivalence that many of them feel toward the Pledge of Allegiance, as well as to understand that American Creed values are ideals—not realities—that we as a nation must work to realize. Students of color, as well as mainstream White students, must also understand (1) that they have a personal role to play in helping to make American democratic ideals a reality; (2) that ideals are never completely achieved in any human society, but provide needed directions and goals for a nation-state; (3) that equality for people of color and women in the United States has increased over time; and (4) that American democratic ideals, such as justice and equality, legitimized and sanctioned the claims and goals of the civil rights movement of the 1960s and 1970s (Branch, 1988).

The nation's students, both mainstream and students of color, must understand that the future of America is in their hands and that they can shape a new society when the torch is passed to their generation. We should help students to dream things that never were and to acquire the knowledge, vision, and commitment needed to create a caring and just society.

3

TEACHING SOCIAL STUDIES FOR DECISION-MAKING AND CITIZEN ACTION

The social studies, like multicultural education, is a field characterized by competing paradigms, diverse approaches and methods, and debates about how social studies teaching in the nation's schools can best help students to develop citizenship skills and abilities (Armento, 1986; Barr, Barth, & Shermis, 1977; Shaver, 1977, 1991). Most social studies educators agree that citizenship, or the development of effective citizens, should be the major goal of social studies teaching. However, social studies educators have conflicting conceptions and ideologies about what constitutes an effective citizen and about what kind of curriculum can best develop citizens for a democratic nation-state (Marker & Mehlinger, 1992). The wide array of social studies scope and sequence schemes and plans that have been proposed for the field reflects the disagreements and tensions within it (Bragaw, 1986). The November/December 1986 issue of *Social Education*, the leading journal in the field, contains a range of scope and sequence proposals.

A number of writers have developed typologies that categorize the diverse approaches and traditions in the social studies. One of the most frequently cited typologies is the one developed by Barr, Barth, and Shermis (1977). They categorize the literature and theories of the social studies into three traditions: (1) social studies taught as citizenship transmission; (2) social studies taught as social science; and (3) social studies taught as reflective inquiry. In the first tradition, citizenship is developed by efforts to inculcate particular values into students. In the second tradition, it is developed by teaching students the key concepts, theories, and methods of the social science disciplines, including history. In the third tradition, citizenship education focuses on decision-making and solving problems that people face in a democratic society.

The Barr, Barth, and Shermis typology (1977) provides a useful way to conceptualize developments in social studies education. However, like all typologies, its categories are interrelated, not discrete. They do not encompass all of the approaches and developments in the field, especially those that have emerged since the 1960s. Newer approaches that are not explicit within this typology include the interdisciplinary conceptual approach developed by Hilda Taba (1967) and her colleagues, the decision-making and social action approach conceptualized by theorists such as Banks (Banks, with Clegg, 1973) and Newmann (1975), and the critical theory, postmodern approach developed by theorists such as Popkewitz (1977) and Cherryholmes (1982), and based on the work of Habermas (1968).

In this chapter, I describe four major periods in the development of social studies education in the United States. They are (1) the traditional or prerevolutionary period that extends from the time that the National Council for the Social Studies was founded in 1921 until the publication of Bruner's *The Process of Education* in 1960; (2) the era of the social studies revolution of the 1960s and 1970s; (3) the public issues and social participation period of the 1970s and 1980s; and (4) the resurgence of history and the rise of multiculturalism today. Next, I describe what I think should be the goals of social studies education in a pluralistic democratic society and a decision-making/social action model designed to attain them.

It is important to keep in mind as I describe the four periods that when one period ended, the developments related to it did not end abruptly. Rather, many trends and elements from the previous period continued into the next. However, the characteristics of the new period became the dominant ones.

You should also keep in mind as I describe the four periods that social studies education in the United States can be viewed and conceptualized on at least five different levels. They are: (1) research and theory; (2) state and school district policies and curriculum guides; (3) social studies textbooks; (4) inservice development and training programs for social studies teachers; and (5) actual classroom practices. What happens at one level can differ greatly from what is happening at another. For example, you cannot assume that just because many articles and books were being written about conceptual teaching by experts during the 1960s and 1970s that most teachers in the classroom were teaching concepts. As a matter of fact, research indicates that this was not the case. Even during the height of the social studies revolution of the 1960s and 1970s, when conceptual teaching was emphasized by many social studies theorists, most teachers in U.S. classrooms continued to teach in traditional ways (e.g., emphasizing facts and isolated historical events) (Shaver, Davis, & Helburn, 1979).

THE PREREVOLUTIONARY OR TRADITIONAL PERIOD

Prior to the 1960s, social studies was dominated by history and geography. The emphasis was on the development of national patriotism and the memorization of isolated facts about events, places, and people. Yesterday's social studies classrooms were characterized by teaching dominated by textbooks, teacher talk, student passivity, recitation, and stories about the historic deeds of the United States and the glorious accomplishments of Western civilization. An important goal of the social studies was to develop patriotic, loyal, and unquestioning citizens. Consequently, little attention was devoted to the nation's problems for fear that its warts might show, and thus undermine the development of patriotic and loyal citizens.

Because little attention was devoted to the nation's problems or the problems related to the growth and development of Western civilization, groups that were the society's victims and were on its margins received scant attention in the curriculum and in textbooks. When they were included in the curriculum, they were viewed primarily from the perspectives of upper-class European and European American males. Consequently, the struggles, victories, hopes, and voices of groups on the margins of society, such as women, people of color, and low-income people, were largely invisible in the pre-1960 social studies curricula, textbooks, and programs (Banks, 1969).

Indians appeared in traditional social studies textbooks either as impediments to the westward spread of European civilization or as "good" Indians who were allies to the Europeans and taught them how to farm and survive in the Americas. In the first case, Indians had to be removed so that Western civilization could advance, such as the Cherokees in 1838–39. In the latter case, they were celebrated and venerated, such as Pocahontas and Sacajawea.

African Americans and Hispanics appeared in traditional social studies curricula largely in contexts in which they interacted with or became problems for the Europeans in America. Little attention was devoted to African Americans as institution builders and as shapers of their own fates and destinies. Content about African Americans was limited primarily to slavery and to a discussion of two or three heroes who made contributions to society but did not challenge the prevailing social and political structures. In the 1950s and 1960s, those who appeared in textbooks most frequently were individuals such as Booker T. Washington, George Washington Carver, and Marian Anderson. More radical African Americans such as W. E. B. Du Bois, Marcus Garvey, and Ida B. Wells rarely appeared in social studies curricula and textbooks during the 1950s. Most of the content about Mexican Americans in social studies curricula and textbooks of yesteryear dealt with the events that led to the secession of Texas from Mexico and the United States–Mexican War.

When nations outside the United States and the Americas were studied, the emphasis was on the study of European nations, with little attention to nations in Asia and Africa. There was little emphasis on active learning strategies, teaching students to question what they read or viewed, critical thinking, or social action and participation.

THE EXPANDING COMMUNITIES OF HUMANS

Over the last 70 years, a rather standardized social studies curriculum has developed in the elementary and secondary schools in the United States, with history and geography dominating during most of this period. In the primary grades, students studied the communities closest to their experiences, such as the family, the school, the neighborhood, and the state. In the middle and upper grades, students studied communities farther away from their immediate experiences, such as the state, the region, other nations in the Americas, and finally other nations in the world, including Europe, Africa, and Asia.

The concept of studying communities close to the child first and more remote ones later became the dominant curriculum pattern in social studies. Paul R. Hanna (1963) of Stanford University helped to popularize this pattern, which became known as *the expanding communities of humans* framework. It has remained tenacious throughout all periods of social studies curriculum reform and is the most common framework in the United States today. When Superka and his colleagues studied social studies education in the United States in 1980 (Superka, Hawke, & Morrissett, 1980), they found that the topics listed below were the most frequently taught at the grade levels indicated. This sequence is very similar to Hanna's expanding communities of humans pattern.

Grade	Topic
K	Self, school, community, home
1	Families
2	Neighborhoods
3	Communities
4	State history, geographic regions
5	U.S. history
6	World cultures, Western hemisphere
7	World geography or history
8	American history
9	Civics or world cultures
10	American history
11	American government

THE SOCIAL STUDIES REVOLUTION
OF THE 1960S AND 1970S

In September 1959 about 35 scientists, scholars, and educators gathered at the Woods Hole conference center in Massachusetts to discuss how science education might be improved in the nation's schools. Based on this 10-

day meeting of eminent American scholars and educators, Jerome Bruner (1960) wrote *The Process of Education*, a book that was destined to revolutionize thinking about teaching and learning not only in the sciences but in all subject areas, including the social studies. In it, Bruner presented his now-famous contention: "Experience over the past decade points to the fact that our schools may be wasting precious years by postponing the teaching of many important subjects on the ground that they are too difficult . . . *the foundations of any subject can be taught to anybody at any age in some form*" (p. 12; emphasis added).

Bruner also argued that the fundamentals of every discipline can be reduced to its *structure*, by which he meant its key concepts, its key generalizations and principles, key questions that the discipline asks, and its unique modes of inquiry or investigation. Bruner stated that the structure of each discipline could be identified and that this structure could be taught to all students in some form, regardless of their ages or stages of development.

By stating that the key ideas of each discipline could be identified and by arguing that these key ideas could be taught to young children, Bruner seriously challenged the leading ideas of developmental psychologists at the time as well as the existing social studies curriculum that was institutionalized in the United States and that had been popularized in the writings of Hanna (1963). The expanding communities of humans framework is strongly based on developmental ideas, (e.g., children should study the family before they study the larger community).

Based on the idea of the structures of the disciplines and other key ideas set forth in *The Process of Education*, social scientists such as historians, geographers, sociologists, anthropologists, and political scientists became heavily involved in the development of social studies curriculum projects during the 1960s and 1970s. Major goals of these projects included helping students to:

1. Learn the structures of the social science disciplines
2. Learn the methods that social scientists used to gather data and study society and how to use these methods
3. Learn key concepts and generalizations in each of the social science disciplines
4. Become actively involved in social studies learning.

Bruner was personally involved in one of these projects, designed to teach anthropology to elementary school students, called *Man: A Course of Study*. Bruner (cited in Dow, 1969) described the emphasis in the course:

> The content of the course is man: his nature as a species, the forces that shaped and continue to shape his humanity. Three questions recur throughout: What is

human about human beings? How did they get that way? How can they be made more so? (p. 4)

In order to develop a better understanding of what makes people human, the students start by studying the salmon, herring gulls, and baboons. The Netsilik Eskimo is studied as an example of a human culture. The course consists of a wide variety of instructional materials, including films that were made especially for the project. The course deals primarily with the first question raised in the quote from Bruner above.

Like any educational movement that tries to change the schools from the outside, the social studies revolution of the 1960s and 1970s had mixed results. It created vigorous discussion, debate, and innovation in the social studies and had some significant influence on social studies curriculum development at the state and school district levels and on textbook writing. It also had a significant influence on the research, teaching, and writing of social studies literature by scholars and university professors.

However, the influence of the *new social studies*, as it was called, on classroom teachers and actual classroom practice was far less than its architects had envisioned. Most of the social studies projects of the 1960s and 1970s were conceptualized by academics and scholars who taught at universities; few classroom teachers were involved in their creation. Consequently, many teachers had a difficult time understanding and using many of the materials and did not believe that they withstood the test of the classroom. Many of the project materials also required extensive inservice training and staff development. Some of the programs, however, such as *Man: A Course of Study* and Senesh's economics program for the elementary grades, *Our Working World* (which was published as a textbook series), became quite popular.

There are probably many complex reasons why schools largely resisted the social studies curriculum reforms of the 1960s. The curriculum reformers erred when they assumed that they could create teacher-proof materials and engineer a social studies curriculum revolution from outside of the school culture. Teacher development and involvement are essential to the effective implementation of curriculum reforms and projects. This basic principle of curriculum reform was largely ignored by the social scientists who led most of the social studies curriculum projects of the 1960s.

These social scientists neither understood nor fully appreciated the complex culture of the school. Schools have a culture that has its own ethos, symbols, norms, values, and traditions. Like other cultures and institutions, a school is not easily changed or reformed, especially by outsiders who neither understand nor appreciate its culture and institutional structure. Probably the most important reason that the social studies curriculum reforms of the 1960s failed to become institutionalized on a large scale is the tremendous holding power and tenacity of the culture of the school (Cuban, 1991).

THE PUBLIC ISSUES AND SOCIAL PARTICIPATION PERIOD OF THE 1970S AND 1980S

Between 1960 and 1980 social movements that pushed for civil rights and social reform were prominent in the United States. These movements included the quests for the rights of groups of color such as African Americans and Hispanics, the rights of women, the rights of persons who are disabled, and protest over the war in Vietnam. During this period, the United States enacted some of its most enlightened legislation protecting the rights of women, people of color, and people who are disabled, including the Civil Rights Act of 1964, the Bilingual Education Act in 1968 (Title VII of the Elementary and Secondary Education Act), and Public Law 94-142 in 1975, the Education for All Handicapped Children Act.

During the 1970s and 1980s the social reform and civil rights movements influenced the social studies curriculum. Many theorists began to criticize Bruner's structuralist position and to argue that it was not sufficient to teach students the key ideas and methods of the social sciences. Bruner's critics argued that the main goal of social studies education should be to develop reflective citizens for a democratic society (Newmann with Oliver, 1970; Oliver & Shaver 1966). To become effective citizens, students needed to learn how to apply social science knowledge to the solution of social problems in society, such as racial discrimination, discrimination against women, and the improvement and protection of the environment. These citizenship and public issues curriculum theorists also argued that students also need to take social action in order to improve society and to develop a sense of political efficacy.

Theorists such as Oliver and Shaver (1966), Newmann (Newmann with Oliver, 1970), Metcalf (1971), and Banks (Banks with Clegg, 1990) developed theories, materials, and strategies for teaching students not only to master social science knowledge but also to analyze and clarify their values, to identify courses of action to take, to consider alternative actions, and to take actions that are consistent with the knowledge and values they have derived and clarified. Oliver and Shaver (1966) developed a theory of teaching public issues to high school students and published data on the results of their experimental public issues curriculum. Newmann (Newmann with Oliver, 1970) developed theories and strategies for involving students in social action and civic participation. In its *Curriculum Guidelines for the Social Studies* published in 1979, the National Council for the Social Studies stated,

Extensive involvement by students of all ages in their community is essential. . . . The involvement may take the form of observation or information-seeking, attending meetings, and interviews. It may take the form of political campaigning, community service or improvement, or even responsible demonstration. The school should not only provide channels for such activities, but build them into the design of its K–12 social studies program. (National Council for the Social Studies, 1979, p. 266)

THE RESURGENCE OF HISTORY AND
THE RISE OF MULTICULTURALISM

The current period of social studies education in the United States is characterized by diverse and conflicting trends. One major development is the resurgence of what is called "back to the basics," which is a return to an emphasis on history and geography that was dominant during the prerevolutionary period described above. This trend grew out of the criticisms by popular writers, sometimes joined by academics such as historians, who argue that students do not know the basic facts about U.S. history, such as when the Constitution was ratified or when the Civil War occurred.

Hirsch (1987) made this argument in his highly successful and widely reviewed book *Cultural Literacy: What Every American Needs To Know*, which was on the *New York Times* best-seller list for almost six months. Its popularity indicated that it articulated important concerns among U.S. citizens about what students were learning in school. Another popular book by Hirsch, Kett, and Trefil (1988), *The Dictionary of Cultural Literacy: What Every American Needs to Know*, also became a best-seller. Ravitch and Finn (1987) extended the argument developed by Hirsch in *What Do Our 17-Year Olds Know?* They describe how students gave many incorrect answers to multiple-choice test items that assessed their recall of factual knowledge in history and literature. Ravitch has argued that the replacement of history teaching with the teaching of social studies is the main reason why students do not know the basic facts about history and geography. Writers such as Ravitch, Finn, and Hirsch think that the teaching of factual history should be emphasized in the schools. The framework developed and adopted by the state of California, our largest state with over 30 million people, is history-oriented and incorporates many of Ravitch's ideas (California State Department of Education, 1987). She was one of the major writers of the California curriculum framework.

Another major development in U.S. social studies education today is inconsistent with the emphasis on factual history. There is a trend to infuse multicultural content and perspectives into the social studies curriculum. A multicultural social studies curriculum describes concepts, events, and ideas not only from the point of view of mainstream Americans but also from the perspectives of ethnic groups of color such as African Americans and Hispanics as well as from the perspectives of women (Banks, 1991b). Major school districts such as those in Portland, Oregon, and New York City have adopted guidelines for infusing multicultural content into all areas of the school curriculum, including the social studies. State departments of education, such as those in Washington and New York, also have developed guidelines in multicultural education. In July 1989, the State Education Department in New York published a social studies curriculum document recommending ways to make the curriculum multicultural, *A Curriculum for Inclusion* (New York State Department of Education, 1989). The publication of this report evoked a major national debate in the nation's newspapers and magazines that indicated that Americans are rather sharply divided on how to describe the balance between national unity and ethnic diversity in the school curriculum. Another document published by the New York State Department of Education (1991), more moderate in tone and language than the earlier document, also evoked considerable controversy and debate in the popular press.

Multicultural education is a growing development in the nation and will increasingly become integrated into the social studies curriculum in future years. Many of the nation's most prestigious colleges and universities, such as Stanford, the University of California–Berkeley, the University of Wisconsin–Madison, and the University of Minnesota–Twin Cities, require all of their undergraduate students to take courses in ethnic studies. A major factor that is stimulating the growth of multicultural education in the United States is the nation's changing demographics (Banks, 1991b), described in the first chapter of this book.

The growing awareness among educators that the knowledge, attitudes, and skills that comprise multicultural education are needed to keep our society democratic and free is another factor that is contributing to the growth of multicultural education. Multicultural education is an education for freedom in three important senses: (1) It enables students to freely affirm their ethnic, racial, and cultural identities; (2) it provides students with the freedom to function beyond their ethnic and cultural boundaries; and (3) it helps students to develop the commitment and skills needed to participate in personal, social, and civic action that will make our nation and world more democratic and free (Banks, 1991–1992).

TEACHING DECISION-MAKING AND SOCIAL ACTION

I have developed a model for teaching decision-making and social action to students in the elementary and high school grades. This model, summarized in Figure 3.1, assumes that the main goal of the social studies is to help stu-

Figure 3.1 The Decision-Making Process

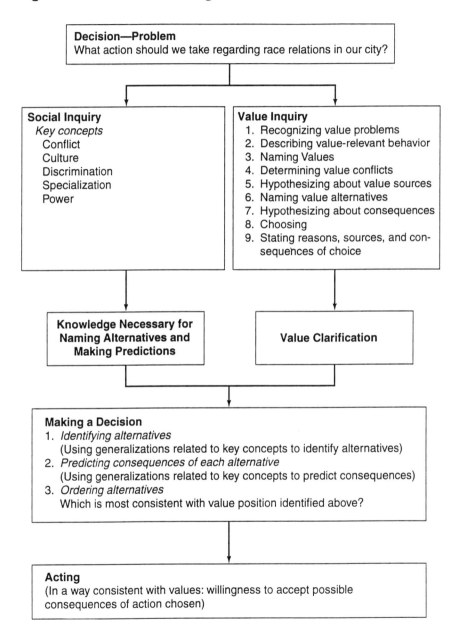

Decision—Problem
What action should we take regarding race relations in our city?

Social Inquiry
Key concepts
  Conflict
  Culture
  Discrimination
  Specialization
  Power

Value Inquiry
1. Recognizing value problems
2. Describing value-relevant behavior
3. Naming Values
4. Determining value conflicts
5. Hypothesizing about value sources
6. Naming value alternatives
7. Hypothesizing about consequences
8. Choosing
9. Stating reasons, sources, and consequences of choice

**Knowledge Necessary for
Naming Alternatives and
Making Predictions**

Value Clarification

Making a Decision
1. *Identifying alternatives*
   (Using generalizations related to key concepts to identify alternatives)
2. *Predicting consequences of each alternative*
   (Using generalizations related to key concepts to predict consequences)
3. *Ordering alternatives*
   Which is most consistent with value position identified above?

Acting
(In a way consistent with values: willingness to accept possible
consequences of action chosen)

Reprinted by permission from J. A. Banks, with A. A. Clegg, Jr., *Teaching Strategies for the Social
Studies: Inquiry, Valuing, and Decision-Making* (4ᵗʰ ed.). White Plains, NY: Longman, 1990, p. 457.

dents acquire the knowledge, skills, and values needed to make reflective personal and public decisions so that they can take action—consistent with American Creed values such as equality, justice, and human dignity—that will improve and reform society. One essential component of decision-making is *knowledge*.

Knowledge for Reflective Decision-Making

There are many different types of knowledge and ways of validating beliefs and observations. To make reflective decisions, knowledge must have certain characteristics. Knowledge that forms the basis of reflective decisions must be scientific knowledge (i.e., it must be derived using a process that can be replicated by others, and it must be public as opposed to private). Knowledge used in reflective decisions must also reflect the experiences and perspectives of a wide range of groups within a pluralistic society. Knowledge that only reflects elite groups within society, or that ignores the perceptions and experiences of various racial, ethnic, and gender groups, cannot result in decisions that reflect the best interests of the commonwealth or civic community.

There are various kinds of knowledge and paradigms, as Kuhn (1970) points out in *The Structure of Scientific Revolutions*. Some knowledge and paradigms challenge the current social structure and support reform of institutions; other knowledge and paradigms reinforce the prevailing social-class structure and institutional arrangements in society. Kuhn also describes how difficult it is for new knowledge systems or paradigms to challenge or replace existing ones. When this occurs, Kuhn states that a scientific revolution has taken place.

There are ample examples in our society of paradigms, theories, and concepts, created by elite social scientists, that have resulted in decisions and policies that have been detrimental to people of color such as African Americans, Hispanics, and American Indians. Such paradigms and theories include Phillips's (1918) conception of the contented slave, Jensen's (1969) theory of the intellectual abilities of African Americans, and conceptions about culturally deprived children that were developed in the 1960s (Riessman, 1962). The cultural deprivation concept has reemerged in the 1990s in the form of *at-risk* students (Richardson, 1990). The at-risk and culturally deprived concepts are not identical, but they are similar in several important ways. Both are labels that tend to blame the victims for their situations; both are also terms that become stigmas for the individuals and groups who are labeled with them.

Value Inquiry and Reflective Decisions

To make reflective decisions, students must have clarified and thoughtfully derived values. An important goal of a social studies curriculum focused on decision-making is to help students identify the sources of their values, determine how they conflict, identify value alternatives, and choose freely from them (Banks with Clegg, 1990). However, students should be required to justify their moral choices within the context of societal values such as human dignity, justice, and equality. If students are not required to justify their moral choices in terms of higher societal values, value teaching will run the risk of becoming relativistic and ethnically neutral.

After students have mastered interdisciplinary knowledge related to a concept or issue such as racism or sexism, they should participate in value or moral inquiry exercises. The goal of such exercises should be to help students develop a set of consistent, clarified values that can guide purposeful and reflective personal or civic action related to the issue examined. This goal can best be attained by teaching students a method or process for deriving their values within a democratic classroom atmosphere. In this kind of democratic classroom, students must be free to express their value choices, determine how those choices conflict, examine alternative values, consider the consequences of different value choices, make value choices, and defend their moral choices within the context of human dignity and other American Creed values. Students must be given an opportunity to reflectively derive their own values in order to develop a commitment to human dignity, equality, and other democratic values. They must be encouraged to reflect upon their values choices within a democratic atmosphere (Banks with Clegg, 1990).

I have developed a value inquiry model that teachers can use to help students to identify and clarify their values and to make reflective moral choices. It consists of these steps (Banks with Clegg, 1990):

1. Defining and recognizing value problems
2. Describing value-relevant behavior
3. Naming values exemplified by the behavior
4. Determining conflicting values in behavior described
5. Hypothesizing about the possible consequence of the values analyzed
6. Naming alternative values to those described by behavior observed
7. Hypothesizing about the possible consequences of values analyzed
8. Declaring value preferences; choosing
9. Stating reasons, sources, and possible consequences of value choice: justifying, hypothesizing, predicting (p. 445)

Decision-Making and Action

After students have gathered knowledge, using a scientific process and making sure that it represents diverse perspectives and points of view, they should make a decision regarding actions they may take related to the topic, problem, or issue they have studied. In making a decision, they should use the knowledge they have attained to make a list of alternative actions, to predict the possible consequences of each alternative, and to order the alternatives. They should ask, "Which of the alternatives are most consistent with our values?"

The students should take action only after they have thought carefully about the alternatives, carefully weighed and ordered the alternatives, and considered their possible consequences. The action the students take may be *personal*, *social*, or *civic*. One possible form of action is inaction. Lewis (1991) has developed a helpful guide to social action activities for students. Primary-grade children who have studied a unit on stereotypes may decide to stop using words and phrases that stereotype Indians and African Americans. Middle-grade children who have studied a unit on prejudice may decide to read several books on various ethnic and racial groups or to make a friend from another racial, ethnic, or religious group.

Junior high school students may decide to do volunteer work for a candidate in a local election who advocates racial equality after they have studied a unit on contemporary race relations. High school students may design, administer, and publish the results of a districtwide survey on racism, as was done by a group of high school students in the Ann Arbor, Michigan, School District (Polakow-Suransky & Ulaby, 1990). In this ambitious project, the students administered the survey to all the high school students in the district. Their response rate was 57.4%, or 2,006 students. Two of the students published an article based on their survey in the *Phi Delta Kappan*, a widely circulated national educational journal. They also presented their findings to the school board and made recommendations. These are among the recommendations the students made in their report:

- Arranging immediate follow-up activities to the survey—including workshops, class discussions, and assemblies—in all high schools
- Reevaluating the district's policies on tracking, with the goal of discontinuing the practice
- Requiring students to take a course that would expose them to issues related to racial oppression in the U.S.
- Establishing a task force to evaluate the entire high school curriculum from a multicultural perspective and to draw up guidelines for dealing with "racial incidents" involving students and school personnel (Polakow-Suransky & Ulaby, 1990, p. 605)

TOWARD DEVELOPING EFFECTIVE CITIZENS

Social studies education in the United States is characterized by many conflicting conceptions, paradigms, and ideologies that mirror the tensions, value conflicts, and developments in U.S. society. Although social studies educators hold conflicting conceptions about what should constitute social studies teaching, they agree that the development of effective citizens should be the goal of social studies education. Barr, Barth, and Shermis (1977) have identified three major traditions in social studies education, the goal of each being to develop effective citizens. They are (1) social studies taught as citizenship transmission, (2) social studies taught as social science, and (3) social studies taught as reflective inquiry.

Approaches and theories that have developed since the 1960s are not adequately reflected in the Barr, Barth, and Shermis typology. These newer approaches include the interdisciplinary conceptual approach, the decision-making and social action approach, and the critical theory paradigm based on the work of Habermas (1968).

In this chapter, I identified and described four major periods in the development of social studies education in the United States and described a model for teaching social studies that focuses on decision-making and social action.

Social studies teaching, research, and practice reflect the major social, political, and economic developments in U.S. society. Because the social studies deal with the nature of people in society, the social studies curriculum is more likely than other subject areas to mirror the debates, controversies, and tensions in society. The social studies curriculum in U.S. society will continue to reflect the major issues and tensions within American life, as well as mirror the nation's ideals, goals, aspirations, and conflicts. The development of reflective and active citizens who can contribute to and participate in making our nation more democratic and just should be the major goal of social studies education as we enter the twenty-first century.

PART II

Citizenship Education and Epistemological Issues

Democratic societies and nation-states are undergirded by fundamental values such as freedom, equality, and justice. In the United States, Myrdal (1944) called these values the American Creed. The quests for both truth and equality are important values in Western democratic nation-states such as Canada, Australia, the United Kingdom, and the United States. These two values often conflict when researchers construct theories and paradigms—in their stated quests for truth—that promote inequality and oppression for large groups of citizens in the nation-state. Phillips's (1918) history of slavery, Jensen's (1969) research on Black and White intellectual abilities, and Herrnstein and Murray's (1994) book, *The Bell Curve,* are powerful examples of social scientists who collected data and constructed theories that justify the oppression and denial of citizenship rights and participation to African Americans and other citizens of color.

It is contradictory for a democratic society to silence the voices of scholars who promote and endorse antidemocratic ideologies and who produce research that justifies the oppression of specific groups within the nation-state or of those whose research promotes equality. In practice, however, the works of scholars who promote inequality often receive wide dissemination in the popular press, while the works of scholars who promote justice and equality receive little. Schools, colleges, and universities should help practicing and future educators to uncover the implicit values, assumptions, and policy implications of all types of popular, academic, and pedagogical knowledge.

Educators should select pedagogical knowledge and content that empower students from diverse racial, ethnic, cultural, and social-class groups. They should help students to understand and to critically examine all types of knowledge and to become knowledge producers themselves. Only by experiencing this kind of education can students become thoughtful and effective citizens in pluralistic free societies. Part II describes issues, paradigms, and theories that researchers have constructed about diverse racial and ethnic groups and their teaching and policy implications.

4

ETHNICITY, SOCIAL SCIENCE RESEARCH, AND EDUCATION

Since the ethnic revitalization movements of the 1970s, educational reformers and researchers with diverse and often conflicting philosophical commitments and beliefs have set forth proposals designed to improve the schooling of ethnic minority youths and to promote educational equity. The basic values, assumptions, and inquiry modes of these diverse groups of reformers and researchers have rarely been critically analyzed in the social science and educational literature.

The inquiry modes, conceptual frameworks, and basic assumptions of educational reformers and researchers—such as the geneticists and sociobiologists, the integrationists, the cultural deprivation theorists, and the culturally different theorists—emanate from implicit value commitments and ideological positions. This chapter discusses how values, fundamental beliefs, and ideology influence social science research and public policy, and it examines the implicit values of several major theories related to the education of ethnic minority groups.

THE TEACHER AND SOCIAL SCIENCE KNOWLEDGE

Two of a teacher's most important roles are the selection of knowledge for instruction and the design of pedagogy to teach that knowledge. Each of these tasks is important and difficult. The selection of knowledge in the form of concepts, generalizations, and theories is difficult because much of the knowledge from which teachers must select consists of factual statements that are not clearly related to major concepts, generalizations, and theories.

The selection of knowledge for instruction is especially difficult in the social sciences and humanities because knowledge in these disciplines is often undergirded by implicit values, latent assumptions, and ideology. This is especially true of knowledge about ethnic groups, because race and ethnicity are emotion-laden topics in American society. Knowledge about pedagogy is also undergirded by implicit values and assumptions.

When teachers select knowledge for instruction and to guide pedagogy, they are making important value choices. Consequently, it is important for teachers to be knowledgeable about the values and assumptions that underlie the knowledge they use so that they can be fully aware of their own value choices. Teachers can make value choices only when they are fully aware of value alternatives and their possible consequences. A major goal of this chapter is to help educators become more aware of the nature of social knowledge and the assumptions and values that underlie knowledge about the education of ethnic groups in the United States.

SOCIAL SCIENCE KNOWLEDGE AND VALUES

Kuhn (1970) uses the term *paradigm* to describe the "entire constellation of beliefs, values, techniques, and so on shared by members of a given scientific community" (p. 175). The laws, principles, explanations, and theories of a discipline are also part of its paradigm. Kuhn argues that during the history of a science, new paradigms arise to replace older ones, a phenomenon he calls a "scientific revolution." Kuhn refers primarily to natural science disciplines and draws most of his examples from them. It is not clear whether or not social science has developed true paradigms because of the paucity of universal laws, principles, and theories in social science, and because social science is still characterized by many competing systems of explanations. Kuhn (1970) writes: "It remains an open question what parts of social science have yet acquired such paradigms at all. History suggests that the road to a firm research consensus is extraordinarily arduous" (p. 15). Social science has also been able to develop few grand theories that are universally accepted in the social science community. According to Merton, social science has been able to develop only partial theories or theories of the middle range. Merton (1968) believes that it is premature for social scientists to develop grand theories because "not enough preparatory work has been done" (p. 45). He argues that the grand theories in social science, such as the Freudian theory and the Marxist theory, have a number of major limitations. According to Merton, social scientists who use grand theories to guide their research often manipulate their data and findings to fit into preexisting conceptual and theoretical frameworks. This leads to conclusions that are faulty and misleading.

The diverse and conflicting theories and schools of thought that characterize social science raise questions as to why there are perhaps no true paradigms, little universal acceptance of grand theories, and many countertheories and counterexplanations in social science disciplines. The complexity of human behavior, the relatively short history of social science, the nature of social science research, and the influence of values on social science research explain, to a large extent, why social science theory is often diverse, conflicting, and controversial.

Human behavior is much more complex than animal behavior and other scientific phenomena. Consequently, it is easier for natural scientists than for social scientists to develop consensus and paradigms. However, Merton believes that we greatly overestimate the status of grand theory in the natural sciences and underestimate the difficulties natural scientists experience in building grand theories. He writes: "Sociologists sometimes misread the actual states of theory in the physical sciences. The error is ironic, for physicists agree that they have not achieved an all-encompassing system of theory, and most see little prospect of it in the near future" (Merton, 1968, pp. 47–48). The social sciences are also newer than the natural sciences; consequently, they have had less opportunity to develop theories, consensus, and paradigms. Social science grew out of philosophy, which has historically been as concerned with normative as with scientific questions and explanations.

In its ideal and purest form, science searches for explanations and theories without influence from human values and human subjectivity. Charles Sanders Peirce writes about the method of science:

> To satisfy our doubts, . . . therefore, it is necessary that a method should be found by which our beliefs may be determined by nothing human, but by some external permanency—by something upon which our thinking has no effect. . . . The method must be such that the ultimate conclusion of every man shall be the same. Such is the method of science. (Cited in Buchler, 1955, p. 18)

Peirce describes the ideal rather than the reality of science. Science, in the real world, is influenced by the values and the social contexts in which scientists live and work.

The subfield of sociology known as the sociology of knowledge is concerned primarily with studying the ways that the social context influences the construction of knowledge (Berger & Luckmann, 1966). Karl Mannheim was one of the first influential social scientists to describe the ways in which society influences the work of social scientists. Mannheim believed that thinking is not an activity free of group influence and that it has to be both understood and interpreted within the context of society. He argued that thinking is influenced by both the historical time and the social structure and that thought is perspectivistic.

Mannheim used the concepts *ideology* and *utopia* to describe perspectives that emerge from political conflict. Ideology describes the tendency of ruling groups to become so "intensively interest-bound to a situation that they are simply no longer able to see certain facts which would undermine their sense of domination" (Mannheim, 1949, p. 36). Utopia describes oppressed groups that are "so strongly interested in the destruction and transformation of a given condition of society that they unwittingly see only those elements in the situation which tend to negate it" (Mannheim, 1949, p. 36). Mannheim (1949) describes how perspective influences concepts:

> Even in the formulation of concepts, the angle of vision is guided by the observer's interests. Thought, namely, is directed in accordance with what a particular social group expects. Thus, out of the possible data of experience, every concept combines within itself only that which, in the light of the investigator's interests, it is essential to grasp and incorporate. (p. 245)

Perspective and values influence the questions scientists ask, their theoretical frameworks, paradigms, research methods, explanations, and conclusions. These factors probably influence research more in the social than in the natural sciences because humans are usually more emotionally involved when studying questions related to themselves than when studying questions about atoms and amoebas.

Perspective and values are more likely to strongly influence research related to emotion-laden issues than research on issues and problems that evoke few emotions. Because race and ethnicity are highly emotion-laden issues in the United States, research related to these issues is likely to be more value-laden than research on a topic such as the housing patterns and population distribution of males between the ages of 25 and 30 who live in New York City.

Social scientists often reach divergent conclusions when studying issues such as the effects of school desegregation on students' attitudes and academic achievement, the extent to which genetic variables influence the academic achievement of African American and White students, and the effects of bilingual instruction on the academic achievement of Hispanic students (*School Desegregation*, 1976). The generalizations that social scientists have reached on these problems are related to the perspectives, values, assumptions, and attitudes they bring to the research process. The conclusions that social scientists have reached regarding these issues, and the public policies they have recommended, are so divergent and conflicting that only initial perspectives and values can explain them.

ETHNIC SUBSOCIETIES AND SOCIAL SCIENCE RESEARCH

I have argued that social scientists, because of the cultures and/or subcultures in which they are socialized, acquire specific values, perspectives, ideologies, and beliefs that often influence their research questions, assumptions, methods, and explanations. In a complex, pluralistic society such as the United States, which is characterized not only by a mainstream culture shared by all ethnic groups but also by ethnic subsocieties, the work of social scientists is often influenced by both the mainstream society and the ethnic subsocieties in which they are socialized.

Many non–African American social scientists conducted studies of African Americans prior to the civil rights movement of the 1960s—studies that were strongly attacked by African American social scientists in the 1970s. Much of this controversy focused on historical interpretations of topics such as slavery and the Civil War, sociological interpretations of the African American family, and descriptions and interpretations of Black English and African American culture (Bereiter & Engelmann, 1966; Moynihan, 1965; Phillips, 1918). Traditional research assumptions, methods, and conclusions of non–African American social scientists often differed sharply from those of the new African American social scientists during this period. Traditional interpretations often portrayed African American slaves as happy and contented, paying little attention to the complexity and totality of their lives and to their struggle to remain human while experiencing tremendous adversity. Many traditional interpretations of the African American family described it as a disorganized institution that negatively influenced the socialization of African American children. Prior to the 1960s, Black English was often regarded by social scientists as a bastardization of standard American English rather than as a legitimate language with its own phonology and lexicon.

During the 1960s and 1970s, many African American scholars challenged traditional interpretations of African American slavery, the African American family, and Black English that had been made by non–African American social scientists and had become institutionalized in the social science literature and in the curricula of the schools and universities. They developed studies suggesting the complexity of African American slavery, the strengths of the African American family, and the nature and function of Black English (Billingsley, 1968; Blassingame, 1972; Smitherman, 1977). Several scholars also described the importance of Black English in the historic and contemporary lives of African Americans.

Although the research and interpretations of slavery, the African American family, and Black English were fairly clearly divided along ideological lines (that is, whether the researchers were assimilationists or pluralists), they were not consistently distinguishable by the race of researchers. A few African American scientists endorsed traditional interpretations of the African American family and of Black English, while non–African American ones, such as Eugene D. Genovese (1972), Herbert G. Gutman (1970), and Joan C. Baratz (1970), presented and supported nontraditional interpretations of slavery, the African American family, and Black English, respectively.

The relationship between the race of researchers and their interpretations indicates the complex ways in which social contexts influence social science data and explanations. It is much easier to describe the behavior of groups of social scientists—such as the new African American group in the 1960s and the traditional non–African American group—than it is to predict or describe the behavior of individual social scientists or subgroups at any particular time in history. Marx, another student of the sociology of knowledge, recognized this phenomenon when he pointed out "that particular individuals might not always think in terms of their class interests, that they are not always influenced in their attitude by the class to which they belong" (cited in Coser, 1977, p. 54). However, he suggested that "categories of people, as distinct from individuals, are so influenced" (cited in Coser, 1977, p. 54). The influence of class interests on scholars, as described by Marx, seems similar to the influence of ethnic and racial interests. Individual members of specific ethnic or racial groups frequently promote the overarching values of the nation-state, such as equality and justice, rather than their own immediate ethnic interests. The nontraditional, non–African American social scientists, such as Genovese, Baratz, and Gutman, supported public policies in their research in the 1960s and 1970s that were highly consistent with the interests of low-status ethnic groups and with American ideals of justice and equality.

SOCIAL SCIENCE RESEARCH AND PUBLIC POLICY

The influence of the social context on the work of social scientists creates complex problems in a field such as multicultural education, which is not only interdisciplinary (and consequently inherits debates and controversies from a number of disciplines) but is also a policy discipline with a particular set of goals. Therefore values not only influence the research in the field, but policy makers influence which research studies get support and public attention and, consequently, influence the nature of the research process itself. Research with different values, assumptions, and outcomes is given visibility and high rewards in different times, depending on the ideologies of the individuals and groups that have the most political and economic influence.

During the 1950s and 1960s, a civil rights movement emerged that highlighted the social, economic, and political discrimination that African Americans were experiencing in American life and called for a redress of these injustices. Social science research that supported equity for African Americans became highly visible and was influential in shaping public policy.

The most noted example of the influence of social science research on public policy during this period is the citation in the historic Supreme Court decision in *Brown v. Board of Education* (1954) of research documenting the negative psychological effects that racism has on African American children. The Court ruled that segregated educational facilities are "inherently unequal" because of the psychological harm they cause African American children and youths. Chief Justice Warren, for the Court, wrote, "To separate them [African American children] from others of similar age and qualifications solely because of their race generates a feeling of inferiority as to their status in the community that may affect their hearts and minds in a way unlikely ever to be undone (*Brown v. Board of Education*, 1954). The now-famous footnote 11, which contains the social science citations, includes works by Clark, Witmer and Kotinsky, Deutscher and Chein, Frazier, and Myrdal.

A range of studies published between 1960 and 1980 supported more liberal policies toward African American and other ethnic minority groups. These studies emphasized the importance of school desegregation for student achievement and positive racial attitudes, the ways in which teacher attitudes and expectations influence student achievement and behavior, the positive aspects of African American family life, and the functional characteristics of ethnic minority languages, such as Black English and Spanish (Comer, 1980; Rist, 1978; U.S. Commission on Civil Rights, 1967). The findings of this series of studies suggested that institutions such as schools had a major responsibility to help improve the education of ethnic minority and poor youths, and that the quality of schools was a significant factor in determining whether or not minority-group students achieved well in school. These studies also suggested a substantial role for the federal government in the education of poor and ethnic youths. One of their basic implications was that the federal government had a major responsibility to help all youths experience equal educational opportunities. These studies implied that the federal government not only had a responsibility to help poor and minority youths to achieve, but that schools could be reformed in ways that would enable them to achieve this goal. Many of these studies, which presented new perspectives on ethnic life and culture, were conducted by the African American intelligentsia. They included Smitherman's (1977) research on African American language, R. L. Williams's (1971) work on African American intelligence, and Billingsley's (1968) study of the African American family. Many studies in this genre, however, were conducted by non–African American social scientists, such as Pettigrew (1964), Leacock (1969), and Valentine (1968).

THE LIMITATION OF SCHOOL THEORISTS

It would be misleading to suggest or imply that only studies that supported liberal policies and a substantial role for the federal government in the education of ethnic groups were published during the time of the civil rights movement of the 1960s and 1970s. Several important and influential studies appeared which suggested that the school was limited in its ability to increase equality for poor youths either because of the nature of class stratification in American society or because of the genetic characteristics of ethnic minority students.

Jensen's (1969) controversial study of African American and White intelligence appeared in the prestigious *Harvard Educational Review* during the height of the movement to secure more rights for African Americans and other ethnic groups. His study indicated that the genetic characteristics of African Americans were the most important reason that compensatory educational programs, designed to increase the IQ of African American youths, had not been more successful. The publication of Jensen's study at a time when a liberal ideology was being widely voiced in the nation suggests the complex relationship among science, values, research, and public policy in a democratic, pluralistic nation such as the United States.

In a pluralistic society in which freedom of speech, academic freedom, and the quest for truth—no matter where it leads—are important and publicly affirmed values, there can and does emerge research that contradicts other overarching social values such as justice, human dignity, and equal educational opportunity. Thus the publication of Jensen's research was justified on the grounds that Jensen was involved in a scholarly quest for truth about the relationship between race and intelligence. In this instance, the quest for truth was a higher value for the editors of the *Harvard Educational Review* than the possible role that Jensen's study might play in denying African American children equal educational opportunities. The editors believed that their primary responsibility, after publishing the Jensen study, was to allow other scholars opportunities to respond to it. They devoted 123 pages of the journal to the Jensen study, which was unprecedented in the recent history of the journal. In their introduction to the Jensen study, the editors wrote: "Because of the controversial nature of Dr. Jensen's article, the Spring Issue of the *Review* will include a discussion of the article by five psychologists" (Jensen, 1969, p. 2).

Stanley M. Elam (1972), the editor of the influential and widely circulated education journal, *Phi Delta Kappan*, published an article by William Shockley (1972), a Stanford engineer professor, who argued that Blacks are genetically inferior to Whites. Elam published an article by N. L. Gage (1972) in the same issue of the *Kappan*. Gage, a respected Stanford professor of education and psychology, presented arguments and data that refuted Shockley's claims. Elam wrote:

> We hope that *Kappan* readers of all persuasions will view the Shockley–Gage encounter as what we have tried to make it: an examination of the questions

fundamental to enlightened educational policy. . . . Even in a period of great racial tension, the investigation must proceed. (p. 297)

The editors of the *Atlantic Monthly* published a highly controversial article by Richard J. Herrnstein in September 1971 (Herrnstein, 1971). Herrnstein, a Harvard psychology professor, argued that "social classes reflect genetic differences" (Herrnstein, 1973, p. 14). Herrnstein's hypothesis differed from Jensen's and Shockley's because he suggested that social class rather than race was related to heredity. Because non-White ethnic groups are disproportionately represented in the lower classes, however, many of his readers called his hypothesis racist. As a result of publishing his unorthodox views, Herrnstein was publicly ridiculed, physically harassed, unable to deliver a public lecture at the University of Iowa, and forced to cancel a lecture at Princeton. It is possible that Herrnstein's views were more vigorously attacked than Jensen's and Shockley's because he argued that social class rather than race was related to heredity. Thus his views can be used to justify antiegalitarian public policies for Whites as well as for African Americans.

Pluralistic democratic societies and institutions are often faced with decisions that involve conflicts in deeply held values, such as equality and academic freedom. They have to weigh and balance values that, as ideals, are equally important. These kinds of decisions create moral dilemmas that are difficult and complex. Whether the editors of the *Harvard Educational Review* and the *Phi Delta Kappan* would have made the same decisions if Jensen and Shockley had hypothesized that Whites rather than African Americans were genetically inferior is an important question that can only be speculated about and never answered. It is clear, however, judging from their reactions to the publication of these articles, that few African American academics would have chosen to publish the articles by Jensen and Shockley. Most African American scholars view the research by Jensen and Shockley as threats to their survival as dignified human beings and to equal educational opportunity for African American children and youths.

Jensen's research is based on what many eminent geneticists consider faulty assumptions and logic. It has antiegalitarian policy implications and was antithetical to the frequently articulated liberal ideology of the late 1960s. Consequently, his work triggered an acid debate and a storm of controversy. Shockley, who set forth views similar to those of Jensen but who enjoyed less academic respect in the educational research community, was frequently not taken seriously by academics. However, he made a number of highly publicized and controversial appearances on television and on college campuses.

Jensen, Shockley, and Herrnstein, of course, were not the only academics who published research during this period suggesting that the school could do little to increase the academic achievement of ethnic and poor youths. Other theorists, who were liberal to radical in their perspectives, argued that the school was limited in what it could do to help ethnic and poor students attain equality because the school was not a very important variable in determining academic achievement levels and adult income. Social class, family background, and luck were more important factors in determining adult income and the life chances of students. These theorists stressed the limited effects of schools on the adult life of all students.

Christopher Jencks became one of the most widely known and frequently quoted "ineffectiveness of school" theorists (Jencks et al., 1972; *Perspectives on Inequality*, 1973). He argued that the most effective way to bring about equality for poor people is to equalize incomes directly rather than to rely on the schools to bring about equality in the adult life of students. He suggested that the schooling route was far too indirect and would most likely end in failure.

Jencks's critics were often harsh in condemning both his research methods and the policy implications of his research. They argued that his recommendations would be used to justify a retreat from liberal policies and inaction by the federal government and by school officials. They also believed that Jencks's radical solution to the problem of inequality—the direct equalization of incomes—would be ignored by policy makers because it was neither politically realistic nor feasible (Rivlin, 1973). Kenneth B. Clark (1973), one of Jencks's harshest critics, wrote:

> The Jencks report cannot successfully obscure its arrogant demeaning of contemporary social science. . . . White policy makers generally do not find this type of historical and empirical distortion difficult to accept when the victims of educational neglect are non-White. These social science rationalizations for the benign neglect or malignant rejection of non-White human beings in America both reflect and reinforce the pervasive racism of America. Social scientists, who by their glib, fatuous willingness to compromise the fundamental humanity of dark-skinned children and who by doing so provide public officials with rationalizations for policies of malignant neglect, are not only accessories to the perpetuation of injustices; they become indistinguishable from the active agents of injustice. (pp. 118–119)

THE NEOCONSERVATIVES

During the late 1970s and early 1980s, a neoconservative movement emerged in the social science community that seriously questions whether the national legislation of the 1960s and 1970s and the War on Poverty had any appreciable effect on reducing poverty and increasing educational equality for minority and poor youths (Kirp, 1977; Steinfels, 1979). Irving Kristol,

Daniel Bell, Norman Podhoretz, and Daniel Patrick Moynihan are some of the leading neoconservatives. The neoconservatives also question the extent to which the Supreme Court should be involved in determining social and educational policies. In general, they believe that the Court is making decisions that sharply conflict with public sentiment and the public interest. The neoconservatives are especially disillusioned with the role of the Supreme Court in legally mandated public school desegregation cases. Many of them believe that the Supreme Court is too adamant in pushing for racially balanced schools and that it ignores other approaches that might be used to increase the achievement of minority-group students.

James S. Coleman has been widely quoted by the neoconservatives since he published a highly publicized and controversial study suggesting that Whites usually flee from cities when their schools become desegregated by court order (Coleman, Kelly, & Moore, 1975). Coleman's "White flight" thesis was harshly criticized by the integrationists (Pettigrew & Green, 1976). Neoconservatives doubt the beneficial effects of legally mandated school desegregation on student achievement and student racial attitudes. They also question educational programs such as bilingual education, compensatory education, and current attempts to infuse more ethnic content into the school curriculum.

VALUES AND THEORIES IN MULTICULTURAL EDUCATION

Multicultural education, like the social science disciplines from which it draws heavily, does not have a paradigm in the sense that Kuhn uses that term. However, theoretical schools of thought in multicultural education can be identified, such as the geneticists and sociobiologists, the cultural deprivation theorists, the integrationists, and the cultural difference theorists. It is important to examine each of these theories to identify their major goals and implicit values and to determine the extent to which they are consistent with the values and ideals expressed in the American Creed. Equality and justice are key components of the American Creed. A frequently expressed goal of American public education is to educate all children to the limits of their potential, regardless of their social class, ethnicity, race, or religion. Historically, we have viewed the school as an institution to help all children attain the skills, attitudes, abilities, and knowledge needed to become effective and productive citizens of the commonwealth.

The Geneticists and Sociobiologists

Geneticists such as Jensen, Shockley, and Herrnstein believe that heredity places severe limits on what the school can do to increase the academic ability and achievement of ethnic minority and poor students. Jensen argues that about 80% of the variance in IQ is the result of heredity and that only 20% is caused by the environment. He consequently concludes that social class and racial variations in intelligence must be explained primarily by genetic rather than environmental differences. Geneticists such as Jensen (1969) believe that compensatory educational programs that are designed to increase IQ are misdirected since an "enriched educational program cannot push the child above potential" (p. 2). Sociobiologists also emphasize the role of genes in human behavior. They believe that some human behavior results from genetic makeup and that some elements of human culture are products of evolution (Caplan, 1978; Ruse, 1979). Sociobiologists approach the study of culture in the same way that they approach the study of biological phenomena. Culture is viewed as an extension of the genes and the result of superior adaptive value. Behavior such as incest inhibition, bond formation, sexual practice, warfare, male dominance, and racial and ethnic sentiments are social-behavioral characteristics (E. O. Wilson, 1978; van den Berghe, 1981). Sociobiologists believe that these characteristics are a probable consequence of evolution. As such, they are seen as integral parts of human nature.

Genetic and sociobiological theories can be used to justify antiegalitarian policies and educational practices. Consequently, public policies that emanate from these theories often conflict with American Creed values such as justice and equality. If a child's intellectual capacity is severely limited by heredity, then the school is limited in what it can do to bring about educational equality. The perpetuation of the status quo and the support of an educational elite are public policies that can be defended with genetic and sociobiological theories.

The Cultural Deprivation Theorists

Cultural deprivation was one of the first theories concerned with the education of lower-class students that emerged in the 1960s. Cultural deprivation theorists assume that lower-class youths do not achieve well in school because of the dysfunctional social and cultural characteristics of their families and communities (Bereiter & Englemann, 1966; Riessman, 1962). They believe that characteristics such as poverty, disorganized families, and fatherless homes cause children from poor communities to experience "cultural deprivation" and "irreversible cognitive deficits."

The cultural deprivation theorists, unlike the geneticists and the sociobiologists, are strong environmentalists who believe that the school not only has a responsibility to help poor and minority students to learn but also has the ability to achieve this goal. These theorists assume that the learning problems of lower-class youths result primarily from the cultures in which they are socialized. They will achieve academically if the school is able to compensate for their deprived cultural environment and alienate them from it. Cultural deprivation theorists see the major problem as the culture of the students rather than the culture of the school.

Cultural deprivation theorists assume that a major goal of the school is to provide "culturally deprived" children with cultural and other experiences that will compensate for their cognitive and intellectual deficits. These theorists believe that lower-class children can learn the basic skills taught by the schools, but that these skills must be taught using intensive behaviorist teaching techniques (Bereiter & Englemann, 1966). The goals of cultural deprivation theorists are highly consistent with the historic goals of American education. They believe that the school should help poor students learn and that it is capable of achieving this goal. However, by trying to alienate poor youths from their cultures, by blaming their cultures for their academic failures rather than the school, and by evaluating their cultures negatively, they violate what Ramírez and Castañeda (1974) call "cultural democracy". In a pluralistic, democratic society, children have a right to an education that both respects and values their family and community cultures, as long as their cultural characteristics do not conflict with the overarching goals of the schools or the nation.

The Integrationists

The integrationists are strongly committed to a society in which children from diverse racial and ethnic groups will freely interact, have positive racial attitudes, and voluntarily associate with members of other racial and ethnic groups (Pettigrew & Green, 1976). The integrationists believe that ethnic groups such as African Americans and Mexican Americans can best attain an equal educational opportunity by attending integrated schools. They cite research by Coleman (Coleman et al., 1966) and the reanalysis of the Coleman data by the U.S. Commission on Civil Rights (1967) when they argue that the social class and racial composition of the school are the most important correlates of academic achievement for African American and other minority students. Integrationists believe that the best way to increase the achievement of African American and other ethnic minority groups is to place them in racially integrated middle-class schools.

Integrationists are strongly committed to equal educational opportunities for minority-group youths and to other American Creed values. Their commitment to racially desegregated schools often becomes passionate, especially when they try to defend their plans to harsh critics of legally mandated desegregated schools. Few issues have polarized American communities in recent years more than the issue of legally mandated desegregated schools (Ratvich, 1978). In some communities, plans for desegregated schools have received mixed or hostile reactions from various ethnic groups, including African Americans, Anglos, and Mexican Americans.

Individuals and groups frequently oppose legally mandated desegregated schools for diverse and complex reasons, including fears of racial groups, a strong commitment to the concept of the neighborhood school, a belief that the burden for desegregating schools falls primarily on minority students and parents, and fears that the quality of education in the schools will drop when they become racially integrated.

The research on the effects of desegregated schooling on academic achievement and racial attitudes is conflicting and frequently reflects the perspectives that researchers bring to the research process (Coleman et al., 1975; Pettigrew & Green, 1976). While supporters of school desegregation are strongly committed to equal educational opportunity for all students, they sometimes support policies that do not consistently support cultural democracy for minority-group students.

The Cultural Difference Theorists

Cultural pluralists, biculturalists, and multicultural theorists are distinguishable but can be categorized as one group because of the research assumptions and values they share. Unlike the cultural deprivation theorists, they reject the idea that ethnic minority youths have cultural deficits. They believe that ethnic groups such as African Americans, Mexican Americans, and Indians have strong, rich, and diverse cultures (S. S. Baratz & Baratz, 1970). These cultures, they argue, consist of languages, values, behavioral styles, and perspectives that can enrich the lives of other Americans. Ethnic minority youths, they contend, fail to achieve in school not because they have deprived cultures but because their cultures are *different* from the school culture.

Cultural difference theorists believe that the school, rather than the cultures of the minority students, is primarily responsible for the relatively low academic achievement of ethnic minority students. The school must change in ways that will allow it to respect and reflect the cultures of minority youths and at the same time use teaching strategies that are consistent with their cultural characteristics. These kinds of teaching strategies will help ethnic youths to achieve at higher levels. The schools frequently fail to help ethnic minority students achieve because the schools often ignore or try to alienate them from their cultures and rarely use teaching strategies that are consistent with their life-styles. Cultural difference theorists frequently cite research that shows how the cultures of the school and of ethnic minority youths differ in values, norms, and behavior (Gay, 1981; Shade, 1982). They are strongly committed to helping ethnic minority youths experience educational equity and to protecting their rights to cultural democracy. Cultural democracy guarantees them the right to keep ties with their ethnic families and communities and the right to maintain their dialects and languages, while at the same time developing competency in standard American English. Ramírez and Castañeda (1974) write:

> Cultural democracy, as we define it, states that an individual can be bicultural and still be loyal to American ideals. Cultural democracy is a philosophical precept which recognizes that the way a person communicates, relates to others, seeks support and recognition from his environment (incentive motivation), and thinks and learns (cognition) is a product of the value system of his home and community. Furthermore, educational environments or policies that do not recognize the individual's right, as guaranteed by the Civil Rights Act of 1964, to remain identified with the culture and language of his cultural group are culturally undemocratic. (p. 23)

Cultural difference theorists maintain that every nation needs an overarching set of values and goals to which all members of the nation-state are committed and that there is a need for a national identity that is shared by all ethnic and racial groups. Members of all ethnic and racial groups should also have the skills and attitudes needed to participate effectively in the political, economic, and social institutions of the nation-state, and should be given the opportunity to participate in these institutions.

However, the cultural difference theory also recognizes the need for Americans to maintain attachments to their ethnic communities (Banks, 1981). For many, especially those who are members of visible ethnic groups, their attachments to their ethnic families and communities are strong and important. It provides them with a sense of group identification, a sense of peoplehood, and psychological support. When members of these ethnic groups are provided the opportunities and skills to participate in the shared American culture and in their ethnic cultures and communities, they can make their maximum contributions to the civic culture because both their personal and civic needs are being satisfied and are given the richest opportunities to grow and blossom.

KNOWLEDGE, EQUALITY, AND EDUCATORS

I have described how research related to multicultural education supports a basic principle of the sociology of knowledge, that is, knowledge reflects the social context and times in which scientists live and work. The influence of society on knowledge and thought causes knowledge to be perspectival, according to Mannheim. While accepting Mannheim's basic premise, I described how the relationship between the social context and the production of knowledge and thought in a pluralistic, democratic nation such as the United States is complex rather than linear.

The United States consists of a mainstream society as well as ethnic subsocieties. Each of these social contexts influences the production of thought and knowledge. Important publicly affirmed values in our nation include equality and justice, yet research is often published that is used to support inequality and other values that contradict American Creed values. This happens because intellectual freedom is a publicly affirmed American value and inequality is an important structural characteristic of the United States which public decision makers often wish to defend with legitimate social science research.

Because pluralism and intellectual freedom are important American values, research that both supports and refutes public policies promoting equality usually coexist in the United States in each historical period. However, research that is most consistent with the dominant ideologies of the individuals and groups in power is given the most visibility, financial support, encouragement, and prestige. Scientists who do research that counters the dominant economic, social, and political order are often relegated to obscurity and usually have little influence on public policy. Educators, like social scientists, have perspectives on knowledge about ethnic groups that reflect the social contexts in which they live and work. Educators bring their perspectives, values, and assumptions about ethnic groups to the schools. They are reflected in their instructional objectives, teaching strategies, and classroom behavior. Most educators are not keenly aware of their attitudes toward ethnic groups and the perspectives they convey to their students.

Educators communicate their perspectives, values, and attitudes toward ethnic groups to students primarily through unwitting actions and words. Consequently, it is important for educators to examine not only the knowledge that underlies their curriculum and methods but also their own values and perspectives to determine the extent to which they promote equity and justice for all students.

5

THE PERSISTENCE OF ETHNICITY: RESEARCH AND TEACHING IMPLICATIONS

The low academic achievement of some ethnic minority youths, such as African Americans, Mexican Americans, and Puerto Rican Americans, is a major national problem that warrants urgent action at the local, state, and national levels. The problem is complex and difficult to diagnose because there is substantial disagreement among educational researchers, practitioners, and the lay community about what causes the wide discrepancies in the academic achievement of groups such as African American and mainstream White youths or between Mexican American and Japanese American students. I have reviewed and discussed elsewhere the conflicting explanations and paradigms that have emerged since the civil rights movement of the 1960s and 1970s to explain the low academic achievement of ethnic minority students (Banks, 1986).

THE CULTURAL DEPRIVATION AND CULTURAL DIFFERENCE HYPOTHESES

When national attention focused on the underachievement of low-income and ethnic minority youths in the 1960s, cultural deprivation emerged as the dominant paradigm to explain their educational problems (Bloom, Davis, & Hess, 1965; Riessman, 1962). Cultural deprivation theorists stated that low-income and minority students were not achieving well in school because of the culture of poverty in which they were socialized. The cultural deprivation paradigm was harshly attacked in the late 1960s and in the 1970s (S. S. Baratz & Baratz, 1970; Valentine, 1968). Its critics argued that it promoted assimilationism and violated the cultural integrity of students from diverse income and cultural groups.

Researchers who rejected the cultural deprivation paradigm created a conception of the cultures and educational problems of low-income and minority youths based on a different set of assumptions. They argued that these students, far from being culturally deprived, have rich and elaborate cultures that are evident in their languages and communication styles, behavioral styles, and values (Hale, 1981; Heath, 1983; Smitherman, 1977; White, 1984). These theorists also contended that the cognitive, learning, and motivational styles of ethnic minorities such as African Americans and Mexican Americans are different from those fostered in the schools (Hale-Benson, 1986; Ramírez & Castañeda, 1974; Shade, 1982). These students, therefore, achieve less well in school because the school culture favors the culture of White mainstream students and places students from other backgrounds and cultures at a serious disadvantage. The school environment consequently needs to be reformed substantially so that it will be sensitive to diverse learning, cognitive, and motivational styles.

The Social-Class Hypothesis

While the cultural difference paradigm has provided rich insights with implications for practice, it has devoted little attention to variation within ethnic groups. Learning and other social science theories should accurately reflect the tremendous diversity within ethnic groups such as African Americans and Mexican Americans. While these cultures share a number of overarching beliefs, values, and behavioral styles, there are enormous within-group differences caused by factors such as region, gender, and social class. Diversity within ethnic groups has received insufficient attention in the social science literature and in the popular imagination.

While variables such as region, religion, gender, and social class create intragroup variation within ethnic groups, social class is presumably one of the most important of these variables. William Julius Wilson's (1978) important and controversial book—in which he argues that the importance of race in the United States has declined and that class has created important divisions among African Americans—evoked a stimulating and acid debate about race and class in the United States. Wilson believes that class is a major factor that stratifies the African American community. Gordon (1964) also hypothesizes that class has a strong influence on ethnic behavior. He writes: "With regard to cultural behavior, differences of social class are more important and decisive than differences of ethnic group. This means that people of the same social class tend to act alike and to have the same values even if they have different ethnic backgrounds" (p. 52).

My aim in this chapter is to examine the social-class hypothesis and determine the extent to which ethnicity is class-sensitive. I will do this by reviewing studies on cognitive styles, learning styles, and motivational styles that include social class as a variable. If social class is as powerful a variable as Wilson and Gordon state, then middle-class African American and White students should not differ significantly in their cognitive, learning, and motivational styles. However, middle-class and lower-class African Americans should differ significantly on these variables. Another, and perhaps more likely possibility, is that social class and ethnicity interact in complex ways to influence learning, motivation, and cognitive styles.

PROBLEMS IN STUDYING CLASS AND ETHNICITY

Several intractable problems confront the scholar who tries to determine the relationship among social class, ethnicity, and cognitive and motivational styles. Most of the literature describing the cognitive and motivational styles of ethnic students includes little or no discussion of social class or other factors that might cause within-group variations, such as gender, age, or situational aspects. Social class is often conceptualized and measured differently in studies that include class as a variable; this makes it difficult to compare results from different studies. Researchers frequently use different scales and instruments to measure variables related to cognitive, learning, and motivational styles. Operationally defining social class, especially across different ethnic and cultural groups, is one of the most difficult tasks facing social scientists today.

The nature of social class is changing in the United States. Behavior associated with the lower class 15 years ago—such as single-parent families—is now common in the middle class. Because social class is a dynamic and changing concept, it is difficult to study social class over time and across different cultural and ethnic groups. Many of the studies reviewed in this chapter used Warner's (1949) Index of Status Characteristics, which was published more than 40 years ago.

Cognition and Learning Studies

Lesser, Fifer, and Clark (1965) studied the patterns of mental abilities in 6- and 7-year-old children from different social-class and ethnic backgrounds. They studied verbal ability, reasoning, number facility, and space conceptualization among Chinese, Jewish, African American, and Puerto Rican students in New York City. They found that the four ethnic groups were markedly different in both the level of each mental ability and the pattern among these abilities. In a replication study, the same researchers (cited in Stodolsky & Lesser, 1967) studied middle- and lower-class Chinese, African American, and Irish Catholic first-grade students in Boston. The replication data for Chinese and African American students were similar to the data on these groups from their earlier study. However, the data for the Irish Catholic students showed neither a distinctive ethnic-group pattern nor similarity of patterns for the two social classes.

Burnes (1970) studied the pattern of WISC (Wechsler Intelligence Scale for Children) scores of African American and White students who were upper-middle and lower class. She found significant social-class differences in the scores of the students but no significant racial differences. No interaction effects were found for social class and race. The scores on the subtests for African Americans and Whites did not show a pattern by race or cultural group.

Backman (1972) studied six mental ability factors among 2,925 twelfth-grade students who had participated in Project TALENT. She examined how the abilities were related to ethnicity, social class, and sex. Sex accounted for a much larger proportion of the variance than did either ethnicity or social class. Sex was related significantly to both the shape and the level of the patterns of mental ability and accounted for 69% of the total variance in the shape of the patterns. Ethnicity was the only other variable that showed a significant effect on the patterns. It accounted for 13% of the total variance: 9% associated with shape and 4% with level. The patterns of mental abilities of the social-class groups differed significantly in both shape and level. However, these differences accounted for only 2% of the variance and were considered by the investigator too small to be important.

A number of researchers have examined a variety of learning variables and cognitive functions related to ethnicity and social class. However, it is difficult to derive clear-cut generalizations from these studies. Siegel, Anderson, and Shapiro (1966) examined the categorization behavior of lower- and middle-class African American preschool children. The children were presented with sorting objects, colored pictures, and black-and-white pictures. Lower-class and middle-class children differed in their ability to group only on the pictures. They used different types of categories. Lower-class children preferred to form groups based on use and interdependence of items, whereas middle-class children preferred to group items on the basis of common physical attributes.

Orasanu, Lee, and Scribner (1979) investigated the extent to which category clustering in recall is dependent on preferred organization of the to-be-recalled items and whether preferred organization or recall are related to ethnic or economic group membership. Social-class status was related to the number of high-associate pairs the subjects produced in sorting. Middle-income children produced significantly more pairs than low-income children. Ethnicity was related to the number of taxonomic categories: White children sorted taxonomically more often than did African American children, who showed a preference for functional sorting. Ethnicity and social-class status were unrelated to amount recalled on the pairs-list tasks or to the amount of clustering. Although African American and White children showed differences in organizational preferences, there were no differences in recall.

Rychlak (1975) investigated the role of social class, race, and intelligence on the affective learning styles of 160 lower- and middle-income seventh-grade children who were equally divided by sex and race (White and African American). The researchers hypothesized and found that, for all subjects, moving from positive to negative reinforcement value across lists resulted in less nonspecific transfer than does moving from negative to positive reinforcement across successive lists. They hypothesized that this general pattern would be more apparent for African Americans than for Whites and for lower-class than for middle-class subjects. Their hypotheses were confirmed. The White subjects reflected positive nonspecific transfer across the lists regardless of whether they were moving from positive to negative or negative to positive levels of reinforcement value. However, African American subjects reflected a negative transfer when moving from positive to negative and a positive transfer when moving from negative to positive lists.

Family Socialization

Some evidence indicates that the socialization and intellectual environment of the homes of different racial groups varies even among members of the same social class as determined by an index such as Warner's (1949) Index of Status Characteristics. Trotman (1977) compared the home environment ratings of 50 African American and 50 White middle-class families of ninth-grade girls to the girls' Otis-Lennon Mental Ability Test results, Metropolitan Achievement Test scores, and grade point averages. She found that the home environments of middle-class White families showed a significantly higher level of intellectuality than did those of middle-class African American families. There was an overall positive relationship between the family's home environment and the child's score on the Otis-Lennon Mental Ability Test. This relationship was stronger for African American than for White families. Trotman believes that there is a cultural difference in the home experiences and parent–child interactions in African American and White families of the same social class, and that this difference may help to explain the variation in intelligence test performance by members of the two groups.

Research by E. G. J. Moore (1985) supports the hypothesis that family socialization practices related to intelligence test performance are different within African American and White families of the same social class. She compared the intelligence test performances of a sample of African American children adopted by African American and by White middle-class parents. She hypothesized that African American children adopted by African American families would achieve significantly lower WISC scores than African American children adopted by White families. Her hypothesis was confirmed: The children adopted by the White families scored significantly higher on the WISC than did those adopted by African American families. The 13.5-point difference in performance between the two groups is at the level usually observed between African American and White children.

The studies by Trotman and by Moore support the hypothesis that the socialization practices of African American and White middle-class parents, at least as they relate to intelligence test performance, differ significantly. However, it cannot be inferred from these findings that family socialization practices do not vary within different social classes in the African American community. A study by Kamii and Radin (1967) indicates that the socialization practices of lower-lower and middle-class African American mothers differ in significant ways. These researchers directly observed how the mothers interacted with their preschool children and conducted interviews with the mothers in their homes. While they found that lower-lower and middle-class mothers differed significantly in some socialization practices, "not all mothers demonstrated the characteristics of their strata. Social class is thus not a determinant of behavior but a statement of probability that a type of behavior is likely to occur" (Kamii & Radin, 1967, p. 244).

Cognitive Styles

Theorists and researchers who support the cultural difference hypothesis, such as Ramírez and Castañeda (1974), Hilliard (1976), White (1984), and Hale-Benson (1986), have been heavily influenced by the "cognitive style" concept pioneered by Witkin (1962; Witkin & Goodenough, 1981). Witkin hypothesizes that the learning styles of individuals vary; some are field-independent in their learning styles, while others are field-dependent. Learners who are field-independent easily perceive a hidden figure on the Embedded Figures Test, while field-dependent learners find it difficult to perceive because of the obscuring design (Witkin, 1950).

Ramírez and Castañeda (1974) used Witkin's concept in their work with Mexican American students. They substituted "field-sensitive" for "field-dependent," which they believe has negative connotations. Field-independent and field-sensitive students differ in some significant ways in their learning styles and behaviors. Field-independent learners prefer to work independently, while field-sensitive learners like to work with others to achieve a common goal. Field-independent learners tend to be task-oriented and inattentive to their social environment when working. Field-sensitive learners tend to be sensitive to the feelings and opinions of others. Ramírez and Castañeda found that Mexican American children tend to be field-sensitive in their learning styles, while teachers usually prefer field-independent students and assign them higher grades. The teaching styles of most teachers and the school curriculum also tend to reflect the characteristics of field-independent students. Mainstream Anglo students tend to be more field-independent than ethnic minorities such as Mexican American and African American students.

Although field-independent students tend to get higher grades than do field-dependent students, researchers have found that cognitive style is not related to measured intelligence or IQ.

R. A. Cohen (1969), who has influenced the work of Hale-Benson (1986) and Hilliard (1976), has conceptualized learning styles similar to those formulated by Witkin (1962). She identifies two conceptual styles, analytic and relational. The analytic style is related to Witkin's field-independent concept. The relational style is similar to his field-dependent concept. Cohen found that these styles of thinking are produced by the kinds of families and groups into which students are socialized. Family and friendship groups in which functions are periodically performed or widely shared by all members of the group, which she calls "shared function" groups, tend to socialize students who are relational in their learning styles. Formal styles of group organization are associated with analytic styles of learning.

Several researchers have tested the hypothesis that ethnic minority students tend to be more field-dependent or relational in their learning styles than mainstream students, even when social-class status is held constant. Ramírez and Price-Williams (1974) studied 180 fourth-grade children to determine whether Mexican American and African American students were more field-dependent than Anglo students. Both the African American and the Mexican American students scored in a significantly more field-dependent direction than did the Anglo children. The social-class effect was not significant. Ramírez found that most teachers are significantly more field-independent than are Mexican American students. However, their level of field-independence does not differ significantly from that of Anglo students (Ramírez, 1973).

Perney (1976) studied field-dependence and independence among suburban African American and White sixth-grade students but provides no information about the social-class status of the community. She found that the African American students were significantly more field-dependent than were the White students. However, it was the scores of the African American females that accounted for most of the difference between the races. African American females were the most field-dependent subjects in the study. The females in the study, as a group, were significantly more field dependent than the males. Perney's study reveals that there are significant field-dependence differences between African American and White students and between males and females. However, this study does not help us determine the extent to which field-dependence is related or sensitive to social-class status.

Locus of Control and Motivation

Researchers have devoted considerable attention to locus of control and its influence on learning and motivation (Leftcourt, 1982). This psychological construct is related to how individuals perceive the relationship between their action and its consequences. Individuals who believe that consequences are a direct result of their actions are said to have an internal locus of control, or internality. Persons who believe that there is little or no relationship between their behavior and its consequences are said to have an external locus of control.

Researchers have found that internality is positively related to academic achievement (Leftcourt, 1982). Students who believe that their behavior can determine consequences tend to achieve at higher levels than students who believe that what happens to them is determined by external forces such as luck, fate, or other individuals. Researchers have found that internality is related to social class and to socialization practices (Leftcourt, 1982). Students of higher socioeconomic status tend to be more internal in their orientations than are those of lower socioeconomic status.

Some researchers (Vasquez, 1979) interested in minority education have devoted considerable attention to locus of control because of the percentage of ethnic minority students who are lower-class and consequently tend to be external in their psychological orientations. Research rather consistently indicates a relationship between social-class status, internality, and academic achievement. A study by Garner and Cole (1986) indicates that while both field-dependence and locus of control are related to academic achievement, field-dependence is the more important factor; the achievers in their study were more field-independent. However, when locus of control and field-dependence were combined, locus of control dominated. The achievement of the groups ranged from high to low as follows: internal and field-independent, internal and field-dependent, external and field-independent, external and field-dependent. A study by Battle and Rotter (1963) supports the well-established principle that locus of control is related primarily to social class rather than to race or ethnicity.

THE PERSISTENCE OF ETHNICITY

As the above review of research indicates, our knowledge of the effect of social-class status on cognitive and motivational styles among ethnic minorities is thin and fragmentary. My review of such studies is representative but not exhaustive. This research does not give a clear and unmixed message about how sensitive ethnicity is to social-class status. Some researchers, such as Lesser, Fifer, and Clark (1965), Trotman (1977), and E. G. J. Moore (1985), have found that ethnicity has a powerful effect on behavior related to learning and intellectual performance when social class is varied or controlled. The findings of other researchers, such as Orasanu, Lee, and Scribner (1979) and Burnes (1970), reveal the effects of social class or the effects of both class and ethnicity on learning behavior.

Collectively, the studies reviewed in this chapter provide more support for the cultural difference than for the social-class hypothesis. They indicate that ethnicity continues to have a significant influence on the learning behavior and styles of African American and Mexican American students, even when these students are middle-class. *In other words, the research reviewed in this chapter indicates that while ethnicity is to some extent class-sensitive, its effects persist across social-class segments within an ethnic group.* However, the research also indicates that social class causes variation in behavior within ethnic groups. Middle-class African Americans and middle-class Whites differ in some significant ways, as do middle-class and lower-class African Americans.

While the research reviewed in this chapter indicates that cognitive and learning styles are influenced by ethnicity across social classes within ethnic groups, it suggests that locus of control is primarily a class variable. Whether students believe that they can control their environment appears to be related more to their socioeconomic status than to their ethnic socialization or culture.

Why Does Ethnicity Persist Across Social Classes?

In his important and influential publication, Gordon (1964) hypothesizes that social-class differences are more important and decisive than ethnic-group differences. He also states that people of the same social class will share behavioral similarities. Gordon emphasizes the importance of social class in shaping behavior. His "ethclass" hypotheses need to be revised and made more consistent with the research and thinking that have taken place during the last two decades (McAdoo & McAdoo, 1985).

Gordon's hypotheses are not consistent with many of the studies reviewed in this chapter. His ethclass hypotheses predict that social class has a stronger effect on behavior than ethnicity. However, this does not seem to be the case for behavior related to the learning and cognitive styles of African Americans and Mexican Americans. We need to examine why there is an inconsistency between Gordon's hypotheses and the research reviewed in this chapter.

I believe that this inconsistency results primarily from a major problem in social science research in the United States related to the conceptualization and study of social classes within non-White populations such as African Americans and Mexican Americans. The tendency in social science is to use standard indices such as occupation, income, and educational level to identify lower-class and middle-class populations within these groups and to compare them with White populations with similar occupational, income, and educational characteristics. The assumption is made that social-class groups in the non-White populations and those in the White population are equivalent.

The comparative study of social classes across ethnic groups in the United States creates problems in both theory construction and in the formulation of valid generalizations because significant differences often exist between African Americans and Whites with similar income, educational, and occupational characteristics. The study of the African American middle class is a case in point. Most middle-class White families live in a middle-class community, have middle-class relatives and friends, and send their children to middle-class schools. This may or may not be true of a middle-class African American family. Approximately 55% of African Americans in the United States are members of the lower class (Blackwell, 1985). Many African American middle-class families have relatives who are working-class or lower-class. African American middle-class families often live in mixed-class neighborhoods, participate in community organizations and institutions that have participants from all social-class groups, and often visit relatives who live in the inner city (Banks, 1984/1996a).

Many African Americans are also members of an extended family, which often includes lower- and working-class relatives. Lower-class relatives often play an important role in the socialization of their children. These relatives may serve as baby-sitters for short and long periods for the middle-class family. There is a strong expectation in the African American extended family that the individual who becomes middle-class will not forsake his or her family and should help it financially when necessary (Martin & Martin, 1978). Unlike many middle-class White families, which tend to function highly independently within a largely middle-class world, the middle-class African American family is often a first-generation middle-class family that exists within an extended family and a community network that have definite group expectations for it and strongly influence its behaviors and options. Many of the generalizations made here about African American families are also true for Mexican American and Puerto Rican American middle-class families (J. W. Moore & Pachon, 1976).

THE PERSISTENCE OF ETHNICITY:
THEORY AND RESEARCH IMPLICATIONS

To reformulate Gordon's ethclass hypotheses to make them more consistent with research that has taken place in the last two decades, we need to recognize the persistence of ethnicity when social-class mobility takes place. This is especially the case when an ethnic group is non-White and is a part of a group that has a disproportionately large working-class or lower-class population. Significant differences exist between the individual who is middle-class but functions within a community that is primarily working-class or lower-class and the middle-class individual who functions within a predominantly middle-class community. Taking these factors into account, we may reformulate one of Gordon's hypotheses to read: With regard to cultural behavior, ethnicity continues to influence the behavior of members of ethnic groups with certain characteristics when social mobility occurs. This means that while people of the same social class from different ethnic groups will exhibit some similar behaviors, they will have some significant behavioral differences caused by the persistence of ethnicity.

When studying race, class, and ethnicity, social scientists need to examine *generational middle-class status* as a variable. There are often important behavioral and attitudinal differences between an African American individual who grew up poor and became middle-class within his or her adulthood and an African American who is fourth-generation middle class. Many of the middle-class African Americans and Mexican Americans described in existing research studies are probably first-generation middle class. Such individuals are sometimes compared with Whites who have been middle class for several generations. Generational social-class status needs to be varied systematically in research studies so that we can learn more about the tenacity of ethnicity across generations.

Other Research Implications

We need more replications of studies related to race, class, and cognitive styles. One of the major problems with the research is that various researchers formulate different questions, study subjects of different ages who attend different kinds of schools, use different statistical analysis techniques, and use different instruments to measure the same variables. Important lines of inquiry on problems related to ethnic groups and cognitive styles are begun but not pursued until valid generalizations and theories have been formulated. Lesser, Fifer, and Clark (1965) published a pathbreaking study that described the patterns of mental abilities of ethnic minorities. However, we know little more about patterns of mental abilities in ethnic groups today than we knew in 1965. Neither the original researchers nor other students have pursued this line of inquiry in any systematic way. As a result, the research on learning patterns among ethnic minorities remains thin and fragmented, and provides few insights that can guide practice.

THE PERSISTENCE OF ETHNICITY: IMPLICATIONS FOR PRACTICE

Teachers and other practitioners reading the review of research in this chapter are likely to be disappointed by the fragmentary nature of the research that exists on ethnicity, social class, and cognitive styles. It is difficult to find such studies. Nevertheless, we can glean some guidelines for practice from the research.

The research suggests that students will come to the classroom with many kinds of differences, some of which may be related to their ethnic group, their social-class status, or social class and ethnicity combined. Research suggests that African American and Mexican American students tend to be more field-sensitive in their learning styles than are mainstream Anglo American students. This means that Mexican American and African American students are more likely to be motivated by curriculum content that is presented in a humanized or story format than are mainstream Anglo students. The research also suggests that middle-class students tend to be more internal than are lower-class students. This suggests that teachers will need to work with many lower-class students to help them to see the relationship between their effort and their academic performance.

It is important for teachers to understand that the characteristics of ethnic groups and socioeconomic classes can help us to understand groups but not individual students. All types of learning and motivational styles are found within *all* ethnic groups and social classes. Many African American students are field-independent and analytic; many White students are field-dependent and relational. The teacher cannot assume that every Mexican American student is field-dependent and that every Anglo student is field-independent. These kinds of assumptions result in new stereotypes and problems. There is a delicate and difficult balance between using generalizations about groups to better understand and interpret the behavior of groups, and using that knowledge to interpret the behavior of a particular student. Cox and Ramírez (1981) have described some of the difficulties that resulted when practitioners applied their research on cognitive styles:

> The dissemination of research information on cognitive styles has also had a negative effect in some cases, arising primarily from common problems associated with looking at mean differences; that is, by using averages to describe differences between groups, the dangers of stereotyping are more likely. The great diversity within any culture is ignored, and a construct which should be used as a tool for individualization becomes yet another label for categorizing and evaluating. (p. 62)

Teachers should recognize that students bring a variety of learning, cognitive, and motivational styles to the classroom, and that while certain characteristics are associated with specific ethnic and social-class groups, these characteristics are distributed throughout the total student population. This means that the teacher should use a variety of teaching styles and content that will appeal to diverse students. Concepts should be taught when possible with different strategies so that students who are relational in their learning styles as well as those who are analytic will have an equal opportunity to learn. Researchers such as Slavin (1983) and E. G. Cohen (1986) have documented that cooperative learning strategies appeal to ethnic-group students and foster positive intergroup attitudes and feelings.

Teachers should also select content from diverse ethnic groups so that students from various cultures will see their images in the curriculum (Banks, 1987). Educational equity will exist for all students when teachers become sensitive to the cultural diversity in their classrooms, vary their teaching styles so as to appeal to a diverse student population, and modify their curricula to include ethnic content. This is a tall but essential order in an ethnically and racially diverse nation that is wasting so much of its human potential.

PART III

Citizenship Education and the Dimensions of Multicultural Education

To help students develop the knowledge, values, and skills needed to become effective citizens in a pluralistic, democratic society, the structure of schools must be transformed. Our schools are not helping large segments of the population to acquire the knowledge and skills needed to become thoughtful, compassionate, and reflective citizens.

The dimensions of multicultural education constitute a conceptualization that can be used by schools and other educational institutions to guide reform efforts that will increase their capability for educating effective citizens in a free society. I have described the dimensions comprehensively in several previous publications (Banks, 1994b; 1995a). They are (1) content integration, (2) the knowledge construction process, (3) prejudice reduction, (4) an equity pedagogy, and (5) an empowering school culture and social structure. The first chapter in Part III defines each of the dimensions and focuses on knowledge construction. The second chapter explicates equity pedagogy. The final chapter focuses on prejudice reduction; it describes research and guidelines for helping students to acquire more democratic racial attitudes and behaviors, an important and challenging goal for schools in free societies.

6

MULTICULTURAL EDUCATION AND CURRICULUM TRANSFORMATION

The racial crisis in America, the large number of immigrants who are entering the nation each year, the widening gap between the rich and the poor, and the changing characteristics of the nation's student population make it imperative that schools be reformed in ways that will help students and teachers to reenvision, rethink, and reconceptualize America. Fundamental changes in our educational system are essential so that we can, in the words of Rodney King, "all get along." The nation's student population is changing dramatically. By 2020, nearly half (about 48%) of the nation's students will be students of color. Today, about 31% of the youth in the United States under 18 are of color and about one out of every five students is living below the official poverty level (U.S. Bureau of the Census, 1993).

MULTICULTURAL EDUCATION AND SCHOOL REFORM

Multicultural education, a school reform movement that arose out of the civil rights movement of the 1960s and 1970s, if implemented in thoughtful, creative, and effective ways, has the potential to transform schools and other educational institutions in ways that will enable them to prepare students to live and function effectively in the coming century (Banks & Banks, 1995b). In this chapter, I describe the major goals and dimensions of multicultural education, discuss knowledge construction and curriculum transformation, and describe how transformative academic knowledge can be used to reinvent and reimagine the curriculum in the nation's schools, colleges, and universities.

There is a great deal of confusion about multicultural education in both the popular mind and among teachers and other educational practitioners. Much of this confusion is created by the critics of multicultural education, such as Schlesinger (1991), D'Souza (1995), and Sacks and Theil (1995). The critics create confusion by stating and repeating claims about multiculturalism and diversity that are documented with isolated incidents, anecdotes, and examples of poorly conceptualized and implemented educational practices. The research and theory that have been developed by the leading theorists in multicultural education are rarely cited by the field's critics, who have not seriously analyzed and studied the writings and publications of multicultural education theorists and researchers (Sleeter, 1995).

The critics of multicultural education often direct their criticism toward what they call *multiculturalism*, a term rarely used by theorists and researchers in multicultural education. Consequently, it is important to distinguish what the critics call *multiculturalism* from what multicultural education theorists call *multicultural education*. *Multiculturalism* is a term often used by the critics of diversity to describe a set of educational practices they consider antithetical to the Western canon, to the democratic tradition, and to a universalized and free society.

Multiculturalism and *multicultural education* have different meanings. I have conceptualized multicultural education in a way that consists of three major components: *an idea or concept, an educational reform movement*, and *a process* (Banks, 1993c). As an idea or concept, multicultural education maintains that all students should have equal opportunities to learn regardless of the racial, ethnic, social-class, or gender group to which they belong. Multicultural education describes ways in which some students are denied equal educational opportunities because of their racial, ethnic, social-class, or gender characteristics (Lee & Slaughter-Defoe, 1995; Nieto, 1995). Multicultural education is also an educational reform movement that tries to reform schools in ways that will give all students an equal opportunity to learn. It describes teaching strategies that empower all students and give them voice.

Multicultural education is a continuing process. One of its major goals is to create within schools and society the democratic ideals that Myrdal (1944) called American Creed values, such as justice, equality, and freedom. These ideals are stated in the nation's founding documents such as the Declaration of Independence, the Constitution, and the Bill of Rights. They can never be totally achieved, but citizens in a democratic society must constantly work toward attaining them. When we approach the realization of these ideals for particular groups, other groups become victimized by racism, sexism, and discrimination. Consequently, within a democratic, pluralistic society multicultural education is a continuing process that never ends.

THE PURPOSE OF THE DIMENSIONS
OF MULTICULTURAL EDUCATION

To effectively conceptualize and implement multicultural education curricula, programs, and practices, it is necessary not only to define the concept in general terms but to describe it programmatically. To facilitate this process, I have developed a typology called the dimensions of multicultural education (Banks, 1994b; Banks, 1995a). The dimensions typology can help practitioners identify and formulate reforms that implement multicultural education in thoughtful, creative, and effective ways. It is also designed to help theorists and researchers delineate the scope of the field and identify related research and theories.

The dimensions typology is an ideal-type construct in the Weberian sense. The dimensions are highly interrelated; the boundaries between and within them overlap. However, they are conceptually distinct. A description of the conceptual scope of each dimension facilitates conceptual clarity and the development of sound educational practices. As Gay (1995) has pointed out, there is a wide gap among theory, research, and practice in multicultural education. The practices in schools that violate sound principles in multicultural education theory and research are cannon fodder for the field's critics. Although there is a significant gap between theory and practice in all fields in education, the consequences of such a gap are especially serious in new fields that are marginal and trying to obtain legitimacy in schools, colleges, and universities. The critics often cite questionable practices that masquerade as multicultural education to support the validity of their claims. The dimensions can serve as benchmark criteria for conceptualizing, developing, and assessing multicultural theory, research, and practice.

The Dimensions of Multicultural Education

I have identified five dimensions of multicultural education. They are: (1) content integration, (2) the knowledge construction process, (3) prejudice reduction, (4) an equity pedagogy, and (5) an empowering school culture and social structure (Banks, 1995a). I will briefly describe each of the dimensions.

Content integration describes the ways in which teachers use examples and content from a variety of cultures and groups to illustrate key concepts, principles, generalizations, and theories in their subject area or discipline. The *knowledge construction process* consists of the methods, activities, and questions used by teachers to help students to understand, investigate, and determine how implicit cultural assumptions, frames of reference, perspectives, and biases within a discipline influence the ways in which knowledge is constructed. When the knowledge construction process is implemented, teachers help students to understand how knowledge is created and how it is influenced by the racial, ethnic, and social-class positions of individuals and groups (Code, 1991; Collins,1990).

The *prejudice reduction* dimension describes the characteristics of students' racial attitudes and strategies that teachers can use to help them to develop more democratic values and attitudes. Research indicates that both children of color and White children have developed a White bias by the time they enter kindergarten (Phinney & Rotheram, 1987; Spencer, 1982). Since the late 1930s researchers have been studying racial awareness, racial identification, and racial preference in young children (Clark & Clark, 1939; Cross, 1991; Spencer,1982). This research is too vast and complex to summarize here. However, it suggests that teachers in all subject areas need to take action to help students to develop more democratic racial attitudes and that interventions work best when children are young. As children grow older, it becomes increasingly difficult to modify their racial attitudes and beliefs (Banks, 1995b).

An *equity pedagogy* exists when teachers modify their teaching in ways that will facilitate the academic achievement of students from diverse racial, cultural, ethnic, and gender groups (Banks & Banks, 1995a). A number of researchers, such as Au (1980), Boykin (1982), Delpit (1995), Kleinfeld (1975), Ladson-Billings (1995b), and Shade and New (1993), have described culturally sensitive (sometimes called culturally congruent) teaching strategies that will enhance the academic achievement of students from diverse cultural groups and the characteristics of effective teachers of students from diverse cultural and ethnic groups. This research indicates that the academic achievement of students of color and low-income students can be increased when teaching strategies and activities build upon the cultural and linguistic strengths of students and teachers have cultural competency in the cultures of their students. Teachers also need to have high academic expectations for students, to explicitly teach students the rules of power governing classroom interactions, and to create equal-status situations in the classrooms (E. G. Cohen & Lotan, 1995). Kleinfeld (1975) found that teachers who were "warm demanders" were the most effective teachers of Indian and Eskimo youths.

An *empowering school culture and social structure* conceptualizes the school as a complex social system, whereas the other dimensions deal with particular dimensions of a school or educational setting. This dimension conceptualizes the school as a social system that is larger than any of its constituent parts, such as the curriculum, teaching materials, and teacher attitudes and perceptions. The systemic view of schools requires that in order to effectively reform schools, the entire system must be restructured, not just some of its parts. Although reform may begin with any one of the parts of a system (such as with the curriculum or with staff development), the other parts of the system (such as textbooks and the assessment program) must also be restructured in order to effectively implement school reform related to diversity.

A systemic view of educational reform is especially important when reform is related to issues as complex and emotionally laden as race, class, and gender. Educational practitioners, because of the intractable problems they face, scarce resources, and perceived limited timed in which to solve problems because of the high expectations of an impatient public, often want quick fixes to complex educational problems. The search for quick solutions to problems related to race and ethnicity partially explains some of the practices often called multicultural education that violate theory and research, such as marginalizing content about ethnic groups by limiting them to specific days and holidays (e.g., African American History Month and Cinco de Mayo). A systemic view of educational reform is essential for the implementation of thoughtful, creative, and meaningful educational reform.

Knowledge Construction and Curriculum Transformation

Because of the limited scope of this chapter, I will focus on only one of the dimensions of multicultural education—knowledge construction. In another publication (Banks, 1996b), I describe a typology of knowledge that consists of five types: (1) personal/cultural; (2) popular; (3) mainstream academic; (4) transformative academic; and (5) school. Readers can refer to Banks (1996b) for an explication of each of the knowledge types. I discuss two of the knowledge types below: mainstream academic and transformative academic.

Mainstream academic knowledge consists of the concepts, paradigms, theories, and explanations that constitute traditional and established knowledge in the behavioral and social sciences (Banks, 1996b). An important tenet within mainstream academic knowledge is that there is a set of objective truths that can be verified through rigorous and objective research procedures that are uninfluenced by human interests, values, and perspectives.

Most of the knowledge that constitutes the established canon in the nation's schools, colleges, and universities is mainstream academic knowledge. The traditional conceptualization of the settlement of the West is a powerful example of the way in which mainstream academic knowledge has shaped the paradigms, canons, and perspectives that become institutionalized in the college, university, and school curriculum. In an influential paper presented at a meeting of the American Historical Association in 1893, Frederick Jackson Turner (1894/1989) argued that the frontier, which he regarded as a wilderness, was the main source of American democracy. Although Turner's thesis is now being criticized by revisionist historians, his paper established a conception of the West that has been highly influential in American scholarship, in the popular culture, and in school books.

Turner's thesis is related to other European conceptions of the Americas, of the other (Todorov, 1982), and of the native peoples who lived in the land that the European conceptualized as the West. Turner, like many European scholars and writers, viewed the West as an empty wilderness that was sparsely populated, that lacked civilizations, and that was the genesis of American democracy and freedom. This paradigm and the interpretations that derive from it largely ignore the large number of American Indians who were living in the Americas when the Europeans arrived [Thornton (1995) estimates 7,000,000], the rich cultures and civilizations that existed in the Americas, and the fact that the freedom the Europeans found in the West meant destruction and genocide for the various groups of Native American. By the beginning of the twentieth century, most American Indians groups had been defeated by U.S. military force (Hyatt & Nettleford, 1995). The will of Native Americans, however, was not broken. A renewed quest for Indian rights emerged during the civil rights movement of the 1960s and 1970s.

The *West paradigm* in American history and culture is powerful, cogent, and deeply entrenched in the curriculum of the nation's schools, colleges, and universities. The West paradigm must be seriously examined and deconstructed in order for students to acquire a deep, complex, and compassionate understanding of United States history and culture.

Students must be taught, for example, how the concept of the West is a Eurocentric idea and how different groups in American society conceptualized and viewed the West differently. The Mexicans who became a part of the United States after the Treaty of Guadalupe Hidalgo in 1848 did not view or conceptualize the Southwest as the West; rather the territory that Mexico lost to the United States after the war was Mexico's North. The Indian groups living in the western territories did not view their homelands as the West but as the center of the universe. To the various immigrants from Asia, such as those from Japan and China, the land to which they immigrated was not the West but the East, or the land of the "Golden Mountain." By helping students to view Eurocentric concepts such as *the West*, *the discovery of America*, and *the New World* from different perspectives and points of view, we can increase their ability to conceptualize, to determine the implicit perspectives embedded in curriculum materials, and to become more thoughtful and reflective citizens.

Transformative Academic Knowledge

Teachers can help students to acquire new perspectives on the development of American history and society by reforming the curriculum with the use of paradigms, perspectives, and points of view from transformative academic knowledge. Transformative academic knowledge consists of the concepts, paradigms, themes, and explanations that challenge mainstream academic knowledge and that expand the historical and literary canon (Banks, 1996b). Transformative academic knowledge challenges some of the key assumptions that mainstream scholars make about the nature of knowledge as well as some of their major paradigms, findings, theories, and interpretations. While mainstream academic scholars claim that their findings and interpretations are universalistic and unrelated to human interests, tranformative scholars view knowledge as related to the cultural experiences of individuals and groups (Collins, 1990). Transformative scholars also believe that a major goal of knowledge is to improve society (Clark, 1965).

Within the last two decades there has been a rich proliferation of transformative scholarship developed by scholars on the margins of society (Banks & Banks, 1995b). This scholarship challenges many of the paradigms, concepts, and interpretations that are institutionalized in the nation's schools, colleges, and universities. Much—but not all—of this scholarship has been developed by scholars of color and feminist scholars. In *Margins and Mainstreams: Asians in American History and Culture*, Gary Okhiro (1994) argues that groups on the margins of society have played significant roles in maintaining democratic values in American society because they were among the first to challenge institutionalized racist practices such as slavery, the internment of Japanese Americans, and Indian removal. By challenging practices that violated democracy and human rights, groups on the margins of society have helped to keep democracy alive in the United States.

Transformative Scholarship and the Quest for Democracy

Transformative scholars and transformative scholarship, which has a long history in the United States (Banks, 1996b), have helped to maintain democracy in the academic community by challenging racist scholarship and racist ideologies that provided the ideological and scholarly justification for institutionalized racist practices and policies such as segregated schools, grouping practices, slavery, Indian removal, and the internment of Japanese Americans.

Charles H. Thompson was a transformative scholar, educator, and founding editor of the *Journal of Negro Education*. The *Journal* was established in 1932 to provide a forum for transformative scholars and researchers to publish their findings and interpretations related to Negro education that challenged mainstream research and contributed to the education and liberation of African Americans. In his editorial comment in the first issue of the *Journal*, Thompson (1932) advocated Black self-determination. He believed that the *Journal* would provide African Americans with a vehicle for assuming a greater role in their own education. He stated that "leadership in the investigation of the education of Negroes should be assumed to a greater extent by Negro educators" and that there was "no ready and *empathetic* outlet for the publication of the results of [the Negro's] investigations. . . . Thus, it is believed that the launching of this project will stimulate Negroes to take a greater part in the solutions of the problems that arise in connection with their own education" (p. 2; emphasis added). Self-determination is as important today as when Thompson penned these words. Other transformative journals founded by African American scholars include the *Journal of Negro History*, founded by Carter G. Woodson in 1916, and *Phylon*, founded by W. E. B. Du Bois at Atlanta University in 1940. Prior to the founding of these journals, transformative scholars had few outlets for the publication of their works. The mainstream academic community and its journal editors had little interest in research and work on communities of color prior to the 1960s, especially work that presented positive descriptions of minority communities and was oppositional to mainstream racist scholarship.

When we examine the history of scholarship in the United States, it is striking how both racist scholarship and transformative scholarship have been consistent through time. Near the turn of the century research and theories that described innate distinctions among racial groups were institutionalized in American social science (Tucker, 1994). A group of transformative scholars, such as W. E. B. Du Bois, Kelly Miller, and Franz Boas, seriously challenged these conceptions (Banks, 1996b). The relationship between transformative and mainstream social science is interactive. Each influences the other. Over time, transformative knowledge influences mainstream knowledge; elements of transformative knowledge become incorporated into mainstream knowledge. For example, the conceptions about race that were constructed by transformative scholars near the turn of the century became the accepted concepts and theories in mainstream social science during the 1940s and 1950s. Nevertheless, a group of scholars continued to construct ideas about the inferiority of particular racial groups based on dubious research.

The history of research about race in America indicates that theories about the racial inferiority of certain groups—and challenges to them from transformative scholars—never disappear (Tucker, 1994). What varies is the extent to which theories of racial inferiority—and other theories that support inequality—attain public legitimacy and respectability. Since the beginning of the twentieth century, every decade has witnessed the development of theories that supported racial inequality. The extent to which these theories, and the individuals who purported them, experienced public respectability, awards, and recognition has varied considerably. The amount of recognition that transformative scholars who challenged these theories have received from the public and academic communities has also varied considerably through time.

Prior to the civil rights movement of the 1960s and 1970s, the White mainstream academic community ignored most of the scholarship of African American scholars, most of whom had to take jobs in historically Black colleges. Most of these colleges were teaching institutions where professors had demanding teaching loads and access to few resources that would support and encourage research. Nevertheless, important research was done by African American and a few White transformative scholars prior to the 1960s. But because it was largely ignored, it had little influence on the knowledge about racial and ethnic groups that became institutionalized in the popular culture and in the mainstream academic community. Consequently, it had little influence on the curriculum and the textbooks used in most of the nation's schools, colleges, and universities.

Although it was largely ignored by the mainstream community, a rich body of transformative scholarship was created in the years from the turn of the century to the 1950s, much of which was incorporated into popular textbooks that were used in Black schools and colleges. Woodson's *The Negro in Our History*, first published in 1930, was published in a tenth edition in 1962. John Hope Franklin's *From Slavery to Freedo*m, first published in 1947, is still a popular history textbook in its seventh edition. Scholarly works published during this period included *The Philadelphia Negro* by W. E. B. Du Bois (1899/1975), *American Negro Slave Revolts* by Herbert Aptheker (1943), *The Negro in the Civil War* by Benjamin Quarles (1953), *The Free Negro in North Carolina, 1790-1860* by John Hope Franklin (1943), and *The Education of the Negro Prior to 1861* by Carter W. Woodson (1915/1968).

MAINSTREAM SCHOLARSHIP AND THE SOCIAL STRUCTURE

Prior to the 1960s, African American scholars and their White colleagues who did research on the African American community remained primarily on the margins of the mainstream academic community. Most of the paradigms and explanations related to racial and ethnic groups that became institutionalized in the mainstream academic community were created by scholars who were not members of those ethnic communities. The paradigms, concepts, and theories created by these scholars usually reinforced the status quo and provided intellectual justifications for institutionalized stereotypes and misconceptions about groups of color. An important example of this kind of scholarship is *American Negro Slavery* by Ulrich B. Phillips, published in 1918. Phillips described slaves as happy, inferior, and as benefiting from Western civilization. His interpretation of slavery became the institutionalized one in American colleges and universities, and he became one of the nation's most respected historians.

Phillips's view of slavery was not seriously challenged in the mainstream scholarly community until historians such as Stanley M. Elkins (1959), Kenneth M. Stampp (1956), John Blassingame (1972), and Eugene D. Genovese (1972) published new interpretations of slavery during the 1950s, 1960s, and

1970s. Transformative scholarship that presented other interpretations of slavery had been published as early as 1943 when Aptheker published *American Negro Slave Revolts*. However, this work was largely ignored and marginalized by the mainstream community, partly because it was inconsistent with established views of slaves and slavery.

More recent research on the cognitive and intellectual abilities of African Americans indicates the extent to which antiegalitarian research is still influential in the mainstream academic community. In 1969 the prestigious *Harvard Educational Review* devoted 123 pages of its first issue that year to Jensen's article on the differential intellectual abilities of Whites and African Americans. Papers by transformative scholars who embraced different paradigms were not published in this influential issue of the journal, although the *Review* published comments on the article by other scholars in the subsequent issue (Kagan et al., 1969). Even though Jensen's article occupied most of the pages in an issue of the *Harvard Educational Review*, he experienced much public scorn and rejection when he appeared in public lectures and forums on university campuses. *The Bell Curve* by Herrnstein and Murray (1994), published nearly a quarter-century after Jensen's article, received an enthusiastic and warm reception in both the academic and public communities. The book was widely discussed in the public media and remained on the *New York Times* best-seller list for many weeks. Although it evoked much discussion and controversy (Jacoby & Glauberman, 1995), it attained a high degree of legitimacy in both the academic and public communities.

The publication of *The Bell Curve*, its warm and enthusiastic public reception, and the social and political context out of which it emerged provide an excellent case study for discussion and analysis by students who are studying knowledge construction. They can examine the arguments made by the authors, their major assumptions, and how the arguments in the book relate to the social and political context. Students can discuss these questions: Why, at this time in our history, was *The Bell Curve* written and published? Why was it so widely disseminated and well received by the educated public? Who benefits from the arguments in *The Bell Curve*? Who loses? Why do arguments and theories about the genetic inferiority of African Americans keep reemerging? How do such arguments relate to the social and political climate? Stephen Jay Gould (1994) responded to the last question in a *New Yorker* article:

> "The Bell Curve," with its claim and supposed documentation that race and class differences are largely caused by genetic factors and are therefore essentially immutable, contains no new arguments and presents no compelling data to support its anachronistic social Darwinism, so I can only conclude that its success in winning attention must reflect the depressing temper of our time—a histori-

cal moment of unprecedented ungenerosity, when a mood for slashing social programs can be powerfully abetted by an argument that beneficiaries cannot be helped, owing to inborn cognitive limits expressed as low I.Q. scores. (p. 139)

The publication and public reception of *The Bell Curve* is a cogent example of the extent to which much institutionalized knowledge within our society still supports inequality, dominant-group hegemony, and the disempowerment of marginalized groups. *The Bell Curve* and its reception and legitimacy also underscore the need to educate students to become critical consumers of knowledge, to become knowledge producers themselves, and to be able to take thoughtful and decisive action that will help to create and maintain a democratic and just society. Works such as *The Bell Curve*, and the public response to them, remind us that democracies are fragile and that the threats to them are serious. Fortunately, the work of transformative scholars indicates that the quest for human freedom is irrepressible.

7

EQUITY PEDAGOGY AND MULTICULTURAL EDUCATION

with Cherry A. McGee Banks

The widespread misconceptions about multicultural education have slowed its implementation and contributed to the contentious debate about its nature and purposes (D'Souza, 1991; Schlesinger, 1991). One of the most prevalent misconceptions about multicultural education is that the integration of content about diverse cultural, ethnic, and racial groups into the mainstream curriculum is both its essence and its totality. The heated debate about multicultural education has focused primarily on content integration (e.g., the nature of the canon) and has largely ignored other important dimensions of multicultural education (Sleeter, 1995).

To be effectively implemented in schools, colleges, and universities, multicultural education must be broadly conceptualized and its various dimensions must be more carefully delineated. In previous publications, J. A. Banks (1993b, 1993e, 1994b) has conceptualized multicultural education as consisting of five dimensions: content integration, the knowledge construction process, prejudice reduction, an equity pedagogy, and an empowering school culture and social structure (see Chapter 6 of this volume for descriptions of the dimensions).

In this chapter, we extend the previous work J. A. Banks has done with equity pedagogy by further explicating the concept, by describing how it intersects with and interrelates to the other four dimensions, and by clarifying what it means for curriculum reform and classroom teaching and learning. We also describe the characteristics that are needed by teachers to actualize this dimension of multicultural education in the classroom.

EQUITY PEDAGOGY: MEANINGS AND ASSUMPTIONS

We define equity pedagogy as teaching strategies and classroom environments that help students from diverse racial, ethnic, and cultural groups to attain the knowledge, skills, and attitudes needed to function effectively within and to help create and perpetuate a just, humane, and democratic society. This definition suggests that it is not sufficient to help students to learn to read, write, and compute within the dominant canon without questioning its assumptions, paradigms, and hegemonic characteristics. Helping students to become reflective and active citizens of a public, democratic society is at the essence of our conception of equity pedagogy.

Pedagogies that merely educate students to fit into and to experience social-class mobility within the existing structures of our society—which are characterized by sharp and pernicious social-class divisions and by racial, ethnic, and gender stratification—are not helpful in building a democratic and just society. An education for equity teaches students to master basic skills as well as to use those skills to become effective agents who work to create a just and democratic society. We believe that education in a pluralistic, democratic society should help students to acquire the content, attitudes, and skills needed to know reflectively, to care deeply, and to act thoughtfully (Banks, 1994a).

The implementation of strategies such as cooperative learning and culturally relevant instruction within the context of existing assumptions and institutional structures will not result in equity pedagogy. Its implementation requires that current assumptions about teaching, students, learning, and the nature of U.S. society held by most teachers be interrogated and reconstructed. Equity pedagogy also requires that existing school structures that foster inequality be dismantled. It cannot occur within a social and political context in which racism, sexism, and inequality are embedded.

Equity pedagogy actively involves students in a process of knowledge construction and production. It challenges the idea of instruction as transmission of facts and the image of the teacher as a citadel of knowledge and students as its passive recipients. Equity pedagogy alters the traditional power relationship between teachers and students. Most important, it assumes an integral relationship between knowledge and reflective action. Equity pedagogy creates an environment in which students can acquire, interrogate, and produce knowledge and envision new possibilities for the use of that knowledge for societal change (Banks, 1994b).

Our perspectives on equity pedagogy are guided by these assumptions:

1. There is an identifiable body of knowledge, skills, and attitudes that constitute critical attributes of equity pedagogy.
2. Critical attributes of equity pedagogy can be identified, taught, and learned.
3. Competencies in equity pedagogy can be developed through formal instruction, reflection on life experiences, and opportunities to work with students and colleagues from diverse populations.

4. All teachers need to be able to competently implement equity pedagogy and related teaching strategies because all students benefit from
   them.
5. In-depth knowledge of an academic discipline, pedagogical knowledge, and knowledge of their students' cultures are prerequisites for
   teachers to successfully implement equity pedagogy.
6. Competency in equity pedagogy requires a process of reflection and
   growth.
7. Equity pedagogy cannot be implemented in isolation from the other
   four dimensions of multicultural education described above. It is interrelated in a complex way with the other dimensions (Banks, 1993e).

Characteristics of Equity Pedagogy

Equity pedagogy is a dynamic instructional process that focuses not only
on the identification and use of effective instructional techniques and methods but also on the context in which they are used. Cooperative learning, for
example, can be a very effective instructional technique (Cohen, 1994; Slavin,
1983). However, when it is used without an awareness of contextual issues,
such as status differences among students, it can reinforce stereotypes and
inequality in the classroom (E. G. Cohen & Roper, 1972).

Equity pedagogy challenges teachers to use teaching strategies that
facilitate the learning process. Instead of focusing on the memorization of
knowledge constructed by authorities, students in classrooms where equity
pedagogy is used learn to generate knowledge, construct interpretations, and
create new understandings (Banks, 1993a; Brooks & Brooks, 1993). Students
make connections between the autobiographical experiences of knowers and
the knowledge they create. In classrooms where knowledge construction
takes place, teachers enable students to identify and interrogate the posi-
tionality of knowers and to construct their own interpretations of reality
(Brooks & Brooks, 1993; Code, 1991; Tetreault, 1993). During the knowledge
construction process, students relate ideas and perspectives and make judg-
ments and evaluations. Instead of looking for *the* single answer to a problem,
students are encouraged to generate multiple solutions and perspectives. They
also explore how problems arise and how they are related to other problems,
issues, and concepts.

Like the other dimensions of multicultural education, equity pedagogy
provides a basis for addressing critical aspects of schooling and for transforming curricula and schools. The discussion that follows relates equity pedagogy
to two dimensions of multicultural education: *content integration* and an
empowering school culture and social structure.

School Culture and Social Structure

A serious examination of the culture and social structure of the school raises significant questions about institutional characteristics such as tracking and the power relationships between students and teachers—and between teachers and administrators. The school culture and social structure are powerful determinants of how students learn to perceive themselves. These factors influence the social interactions that take place between students and teachers and among students, both within as well as outside the classroom.

Tracking and power relationships within a school are important components of its deep structure (Tye, 1987). The deep structure includes the bell schedule, the physical uniformity of classrooms, test scores, and various factors that allow teachers to maintain control in the classroom (Tye, 1987). Equity pedagogy challenges the deep structure of schools because its requirements for scheduling, arrangement of physical space, and control are frequently at odds with traditional instructional methods that reinforce the deep structure of schools. If students are going to be involved in the production of knowledge, they need class schedules that allow time for these activities. The 50-minute time slot usually does not allow students the time they need for reflection and content integration and synthesis. Furthermore, students who are involved in producing knowledge may need to work in places other than the classroom. Teachers may not be able to exercise as much control over students who are working in other areas of the school building, such as the library, or at sites off campus.

These elements of the deep structure of schools are important components of the hidden curriculum. When teachers use equity pedagogy that challenges the deep structure of schools, important aspects of the hidden curriculum are often revealed. Becoming aware of the relationship among the school culture, the social structure, and the deep structure of schools can heighten the teacher's awareness of the power of the hidden curriculum, or what P. W. Jackson (1992) calls the "untaught lessons."

The Hidden Curriculum

The classroom is a public site. School teaching and learning take place primarily in groups and through social interactions. Interactions between teachers and students and among students are important parts of the relationship between equity pedagogy and the hidden curriculum. Implementing equity pedagogy requires teachers to understand how students perceive social interactions with their teachers, what they learn from them, and the extent to which students perceive their teachers as caring persons. Equity pedagogy can help reveal the nature of the hidden curriculum by encouraging teachers to raise questions such as: Is this class meaningful for my students? Would my students like a different teacher? Why or why not? What gaps exist between what I am teaching and what my students are learning? If there are gaps, why? If not, why not?

Significant adult–student interactions often occur within the context of the hidden curriculum. The number of people available to work with students in the classroom is an important part of the hidden curriculum. Some classes—often differentiated by social class and designations such as gifted and accelerated—have many parent and community volunteers available to provide classroom help and to implement enrichment programs. The adults in these classes are able to provide students with individualized instruction, often communicating the implicit message that the students are special and important. Teachers who work in schools in which some classes have multiple adult helpers and other classes have only one adult should realize that these kinds of factors can severely limit the effectiveness of culturally sensitive pedagogy and cooperative learning.

When used in isolation, instructional strategies such as cooperative learning and constructivist techniques cannot sufficiently deal with the problems embedded in the hidden curriculum. To transform pedagogy, the adults in schools must address the social-class, racial, and ethnic inequalities imbedded in the differential support given to different classes and schools that are stratified by race, ethnicity, and class. The construction of equity in schools as well as the implementation of culturally sensitive teaching methods are necessary to actualize equity pedagogy.

The physical arrangement of space in a classroom is also an aspect of the hidden curriculum that communicates implicit messages to students. When chairs in a classroom are lined up in straight rows facing the teacher, the implicit message is that all students are expected to participate in the same activities simultaneously and to learn in identical ways as directed by the teacher (Tye, 1987).

Learning centers, on the other hand, suggest that students can legitimately engage in different activities, that they are the focus in the classroom, and that learning can be interesting and rewarding. Teachers who try to implement equity pedagogy without attending to factors such as the physical arrangement of space in the classroom and the control inherent in certain types of physical conditions will rarely experience success.

Students also learn from their peers. Consequently it is important for teachers to understand interactions among students. An important part of school for most students involves meeting and interacting with friends. Students are usually actively engaged in interactions with their peers throughout the school day. Peer relationships are an important part of the social context of the classroom and should be an important instructional consideration. They can become potent elements in dismantling the hidden curriculum. Implementing group work without making provisions for dealing with the status differences among students based on race, gender, and social class may result in marginalizing students from low-status groups rather than providing opportunities for them to learn from their peers (E. G. Cohen, 1994; E. G. Cohen & Roper, 1972).

Students learn about themselves as they acquire academic knowledge. The academic self-concept of students is highly related to their general self-concept, their ability to perform academic work, and their ability to function competently among peers (Brookover, Beady, Flood, Schweitzer, & Wisenbaker, 1979). Equity pedagogy requires teachers to deal with the dynamics of peer interactions in classroom life. Students are not one-dimensional; therefore equity pedagogy has to reflect the complexity of student interactions and relationships.

Content Integration and Assessment

Equity pedagogy is tightly intertwined with content integration. How an instructor teaches is informed and shaped by what is taught. Both equity pedagogy and curriculum influence the form and function of learning (Vygotsky, 1978). Equity pedagogy is most powerful when it is integrated with transformative curricula. Most mainstream curricula do not actualize the full power of equity pedagogy, thus limiting equity pedagogy to incremental strategies that are characterized by ideological constraints.

Required content, however, can be taught using a transformative pedagogy, as was done by a high school physics teacher in a Seattle suburban school. He transformed a unit on torques by asking the students to identify a bridge that had collapsed, to investigate why it collapsed, and to determine how the collapse of the bridge affected people in the community. Working in groups, the students designed bridges that could withstand designated wind speeds and weights. This unit provided opportunities for students to connect their study of torques to a real historical event, to draw on the strengths of their peers by working in groups, and to actively engage in constructing knowledge by translating the information they collected on bridges into new designs.

Transformative curricula provide a rich context for equity pedagogy because both transformative curricula and equity pedagogy promote knowledge construction and curriculum reform. Transformative curricula and equity pedagogy also assume that the cultures of students are valid, that effective teaching must reflect the lives and interests of students (Ladson-Billings, 1990), and that students must be provided opportunities to construct meaningful knowledge. In this sense, equity pedagogy is directly related to curriculum reform.

Information is increasing at an astronomical rate. What was once packaged in a one-volume text now requires two or more. Teachers are increasingly finding it difficult to cover all the information they are expected to include in the curriculum. Equity pedagogy provides a rationale and a process that can help teachers focus on the essence of the curriculum rather than on isolated and rapidly changing information.

Students in the twenty-first century, unlike those in earlier times, will have to address complex issues that cannot be answered with discrete facts. To be effective, students must know where to get the information they need, how to formulate questions that will provide access to the appropriate information, how to evaluate the information from a cognitive as well as a value perspective, how to integrate it with other information, and how to make reflective decisions based on the best information they can construct. Equity pedagogy helps students to acquire these skills.

Equity pedagogy is student-focused. It incorporates issues, concepts, principles, and problems that are real and meaningful to students. Teachers who embrace equity pedagogy assume that all students can learn. They work to develop student potential and to create a classroom environment that is encouraging and filled with opportunities for success.

Equity pedagogy has important implications for assessment. Educators who embrace it must interrogate traditional tests and letter grades. Assessment strategies based on the assumption that all students can learn provide opportunities for students to improve their performances. The teacher who embraces equity pedagogy frequently gives students detailed feedback on poorly prepared assignments and asks students to "revisit" their work. Written comments instead of letter grades provide opportunities for teachers to identify areas of competence as well as to suggest strategies for improvement and remediation. Portfolio assessment also gives students an opportunity to demonstrate their growth over time and allows teachers to give students ongoing support and encouragement (Valencia, Hiebert, & Afflerbach, 1994). Students can use portfolios to document the complexity and individuality of their work and to reflect on their progress and areas that need improvement. Portfolios contribute to sound assessment decisions and to student development. They describe and provide materials that collectively suggest the scope and quality of a student's performance. Portfolios also provide the structure needed for teachers and students to better understand and make connections between teaching and learning.

Teacher Characteristics

Teachers who successfully implement equity pedagogy draw upon a sophisticated knowledge base. They can enlist a broad range of pedagogical skills and have a keen understanding of their own cultural experiences, values, and attitudes toward people who are culturally, racially, and ethnically different from themselves. The skills, knowledge, and attitudes necessary to successfully implement equity pedagogy are the result of study, practical experience, and reflective self-analysis.

Reflective self-analysis requires teachers to identify, examine, and reflect upon their attitudes toward different ethnic, racial, gender, and social-class groups. Many teachers are unaware of the extent to which they embrace racist and sexist attitudes and behaviors that are institutionalized within society as well as how they benefit from these related societal practices (King, 1992). Reflecting on their own life journeys—by writing their life stories—can be a powerful tool for helping teachers to gain a better understanding of the ways in which institutionalized conceptions of race, class, and gender have influenced their personal lives.

Autobiographical accounts and episodes provide an opportunity for teachers to reflect on times in their lives when they were the "other" who experienced discrimination or a sense of isolation because of their race, class, gender, culture, or other personal characteristics. Reflective self-analysis cannot be a one-time event. Multicultural awareness can result only from in-depth work on the self. It requires the unraveling of myths that perpetuate social-class, gender, and racial privilege (King, 1992; McIntosh, 1990) and a commitment to maintain multicultural awareness and action.

Equity pedagogy cannot be implemented in a vacuum. It requires more than goodwill and good intentions. It requires multicultural knowledge, pedagogical knowledge, and subject-area knowledge (Banks, 1991b, 1994a, 1994b; Banks & Banks, 1995b). Our discussion focuses on multicultural knowledge. However, teachers will not be able to use it effectively without a strong background in their subject area and a sophisticated understanding of pedagogy.

Multicultural knowledge includes key concepts in multicultural education such as culture, immigration, racism, sexism, cultural assimilation, structural assimilation, ethnic group, stereotypes, prejudice, and institutional racism (Banks, 1991, 1994a). Students will have opportunities to study some of these concepts in depth because powerful ideas will be the focus of some lessons and units. In other cases teachers will use their understandings of the concepts to weave them into classroom discourse, to help students describe their feelings and experiences, and to draw linkages among different topics.

Teachers must also be able to recognize, compare, and contrast examples of various theories related to diversity, such as cultural difference, cultural deficit, genetic, and cultural ecology theories (Banks, 1994a). Each of these theories has been used to explain poor academic achievement among low-income students and students of color (S. S. Baratz & Baratz, 1970). Cultural deficit theory, for example, has been used to guide the development of many early childhood intervention programs, such as Head Start and Distar. An important goal of these programs is to increase the academic achievement of low-status groups.

It is not uncommon for teachers to select aspects from several theories to guide their work with students. An eclectic theoretical approach may sometimes be effective, but it can also be counterproductive. A teacher who has read the book by Gilligan, Lyons, and Hanmer (1990) on adolescent young women may understand that girls often equate fairness with listening. These teachers might then make a special effort to call on females and males in their classes on an equal basis. Multicultural theory, however, reveals that equity may not always mean treating different groups the same (Gay, 1993); it may sometimes be necessary to treat groups differently in order to create equal-status situations for marginalized students. Providing an equal voice for females may sometimes require an unequal focus on female views and issues in classroom discourse. Equity pedagogy requires teachers to be able to recognize and respond to multiple student characteristics, including their race, social class, and gender.

The effective implementation of equity pedagogy requires teachers to have a deep understanding of the histories, modal characteristics, and intra-group differences of the major racial and ethnic groups (Banks, 1991b). This content and conceptual knowledge can provide a foundation to help teachers design and select appropriate instructional materials for their students (Ladson-Billings, 1990, 1994, 1995a), make informed decisions about when to use culturally sensitive pedagogy, and decide when to focus on the individual characteristics of students (Nieto, 1994). For example, research summarized by Shade (1982) indicates that Latino and African American students often prefer a learning environment that is more personalized and contextual than many mainstream middle-class White students. While the literature on learning style suggests that some learning environments are more appropriate for various groups of students, it also suggests that students from all ethnic and racial groups can be found in each of the categories identified by learning style theorists (Shade & New, 1993). When reading and using learning style theories, teachers should question and analyze them carefully. The learning style paradigm is a complex one that defies simplistic classroom applications (Irvine & York, 1995). This paradigm has been criticized by researchers such as Kleinfeld and Nelson (1991), who believe that it may result in the construction of new stereotypes about low-achieving groups of students.

Knowledge of the histories, modal characteristics, and intragroup differences of ethnic groups requires teachers to look beyond the physical characteristics of students and to consider the complexity of their individual and group experiences. A Latino student's biographical journey, social class, and geographical location may indicate that a teacher should not focus on modal characteristics of Latinos in determining appropriate pedagogy for that student. Instead, the teacher should focus on the individual characteristics of the student. Knowledge of the histories, modal characteristics, and intragroup differences of ethnic groups is necessary for teachers to make informed decisions about when and how to use knowledge about the cultural and ethnic backgrounds of students when making pedagogical decisions.

TEACHING AS A MULTICULTURAL ENCOUNTER

Teaching is a multicultural encounter. Both teachers and students belong to diverse groups differentiated by variables such as age, social class, gender, race, and ethnicity. Equity pedagogy helps teachers to use diversity as a resource that can help them bring meaning to multicultural classroom interactions. Teachers who are skilled in equity pedagogy are able to use diversity to enrich instruction instead of fearing or ignoring it. They are able to use diversity successfully because they understand its meaning in their own lives and in the lives of their students. They are able to analyze, clarify, and state their personal values related to cultural diversity and to act in ways consistent with their beliefs.

Self-understanding along with knowledge of the histories, modal characteristics, and intragroup differences of ethnic groups are competencies required for teachers to implement equity pedagogy. They provide a foundation for teachers to identify, create, and implement teaching strategies that enhance the academic achievement of students of both genders and from diverse racial, ethnic, and cultural groups. Equity pedagogy is not embodied in specific strategies: It is a process that locates the student at the center of schooling. When effectively implemented, equity pedagogy enriches the lives of both teachers and students and enables them to envision and to help create a more humane and caring society.

8

CITIZENSHIP EDUCATION AND THE DEVELOPMENT OF DEMOCRATIC RACIAL ATTITUDES

Citizens in a democratic, pluralistic society must interact and engage in public discourse with people from diverse racial, ethnic, gender, and social-class groups. Civic, moral, and just communities in which people from many different groups can engage in public talk must be created within pluralistic free societies. To create effective democratic communities within a pluralistic nation-state, it is also essential for a superordinate group identity to be developed to which all groups can identify and have loyalty.

Social-psychological research indicates that individuals tend to categorize people into and to discriminate against out-groups, a behavior that poses a serious challenge to creating civic, moral, and just communities in which the acceptance of out-groups becomes normative. This research and theory, known as the *minimal group paradigm*, indicates that whenever in-groups and out-groups form, stereotypes, prejudice, and discrimination develop. It also indicates that when mere categorization develops, individuals favor the in-group over the out-group and discriminate against the out-group (Rothbart & John, 1993). This is the case even though the in-group and out-group may have had no prior history of animosity and conflict. The basis for the in-group/out-group distinctions can be quite arbitrary and contrived, hence the name *minimal group paradigm.*

In a series of studies, Tajfel and colleagues (Tajfel, 1970; Billig & Tajfel, 1973) produced considerable evidence to support the postulate that individuals are likely to evaluate the in-group more favorably than the out-group and to treat the in-group more favorably even when the differences between the groups are minimal, contrived, and insignificant. These studies indicate the power of categorization.

Because of the tendency of individuals to categorize, to construct in-group/out-group distinctions, and to stereotype out-group members as the "other," it is essential that educators—in order to foster democratic schools and a free society—design and implement strategies to improve intergroup relations. Another important aim of schools should be to help construct *superordinate* groups in schools and classrooms. This chapter examines research on ways in which students can be helped to develop more democratic racial attitudes and values and consequently to become more effective citizens in a pluralistic, democratic society.

The studies reviewed in this chapter describe interventions designed to modify the attitudes and behavior of individual students. Modifying the attitudes and behaviors of individuals is necessary but not sufficient (Aboud, 1988; Brown, 1995; Milner, 1983). *Institutional racism*, which is perpetuated by the institutions and structures in society such as the media, the courts, and the economy, must also be an important target in a holistic approach designed to reduce racism and to create democratic schools and a free society. Although a discussion of institutional racism is beyond the scope of this chapter, its importance must be acknowledged and recognized in any effective strategy to reduce prejudice among individuals. A number of important and informative books describe institutional racism in American society, including Omi and Winant (1986), Smedley (1993), Winant (1994), and Feagin and Sikes (1994).

THE MODIFICATION OF
THE RACIAL ATTITUDES OF STUDENTS

The research that describes the racial awareness, attitudes and self-identification of students (Milner, 1983; Phinney & Rotheram, 1987) is much richer than the research that describes ways in which their intergroup attitudes can be modified (Banks, 1991a; 1993d). Only a few research reviews in recent years have described the ways in which children's intergroup attitudes can be modified (e.g., Banks, 1991a; P. A. Katz, 1976; Stephan, 1985). The Stephan review includes studies that had both adults and children as subjects.

The Clarks reported no interventions that were designed to modify the racial preferences of children in their famous doll studies in the 1930s and 1940s (Clark & Clark, 1939, 1940). A few intervention studies were conducted in the 1940s (Agnes, 1947; E. P. Jackson, 1944), but most of these were conducted using adolescent youths as subjects. The number of intervention studies did not increase substantially until the intergroup education movement reached its peak in the 1950s (Cook & Cook, 1954). Most of the intervention studies conducted during the intergroup education movement of the 1940s and 1950s also used older children as subjects. One exception was the important study by Trager and Yarrow (1952) that was conducted using children between the ages of 5 and 8 in kindergarten and in the first and second grades. A cumulative body of research and theory on the modification of young children's racial attitudes did not develop until studies were conducted by Williams and colleagues at Wake Forest University in the 1960s and 1970s (Best, Smith, Graves, & Williams,1975; J. E. Williams & Edwards, 1969).

Several types of studies have been conducted to help children develop more democratic racial attitudes and behaviors. These include the *reinforcement studies* conducted by Williams and his colleagues (e. g., Best et al., 1975; J. E. Williams & Edwards, 1969; J. E. Williams & Morland, 1976), *perceptual differentiation studies* conducted by Katz and her colleagues (e.g., P. A. Katz, 1973, 1976, 1982; P. A. Katz & Zalk, 1978), *curriculum intervention studies* (e.g., Litcher & Johnson, 1969; Trager & Yarrow, 1952; Yawkey & Blackwell, 1974), and studies that use *cooperative activities and contact situations* to help children develop more democratic attitudes and values (e.g., Aronson & Bridgeman, 1979; DeVries, Edwards, & Slavin, 1978; Slavin, 1979, 1983, 1985). Most intervention studies conducted using preschool and primary-grade children as subjects have been reinforcement studies. Only a few perceptual differentiation studies have been reported. Most curriculum intervention studies have used older students as subjects (Banks, 1991a). All of the cooperative learning intervention studies reviewed in this chapter used elementary and high school students as subjects; none used kindergarten and primary-grade children. Each of the four categories of studies identified above is discussed in the next section of this chapter.

Reinforcement Studies

In the late 1960s, Williams and his colleagues (J. E. Williams & Edwards, 1969; J. E. Williams & Morland, 1976) began a series of laboratory reinforcement studies to modify preschool children's attitudes toward the colors black and white, and to determine whether a reduction of white bias toward objects and animals would generalize to White and Black people. One of the first of a series of laboratory experiments was conducted by J. E. Williams and Edwards (1969). The sample consisted of 84 White preschool children in Winston-Salem, North Carolina, who ranged in age from 5 years, 0 months to 5 years, 11 months when the intervention began.

Two kinds of assessments were used to determine the children's color concepts and racial attitudes: (1) a picture-story procedure for assessing connotative meanings of black and white and (2) a picture-story technique that measured attitudes toward Black and White persons. This is an example of the first procedure: The experimenter showed the child a white horse and a black horse and asked, "Which is the good horse? Which is the ugly horse? Which is the clean horse? Which is the stupid horse?" The next example is from the second procedure: A child was shown drawings of two identical figures, one pinkish-tan with light yellow hair (White) and the other medium-brown with black hair (African American). The experimenter said: "Here are two girls. Everyone says that one is pretty. Which is the pretty girl?"

In the experimental groups, the children received positive reinforcement for choosing black animals in response to story sentences that contained positive adjectives, or for choosing white animals when responding to story sentences that contained negative adjectives. The subjects were divided into three experimental groups and one control group. The three experimental groups were (1) positive reinforcement only, (2) negative reinforcement only, and (3) positive and negative reinforcement. The control group received no reinforcement.

The picture-story procedure with animals was administered twice at two-week intervals. The procedure with human figures was administered two weeks after the administration of the second session of the color-meaning procedure. During the administration of the color-meaning procedure, when a child made a "correct" response he or she was given candy in the positive reinforcement group. Two of the 30 pennies that the children had been given were lost when they gave incorrect responses in the negative reinforcement group. In the positive reinforcement/negative reinforcement group, the children received candy when they gave correct responses and lost two pennies when they gave incorrect responses. In the control group, no mention was made of right and wrong answers and no reinforcement was given. When the racial attitude procedure was administered, no reinforcement was given in any of the groups.

J. E. Williams and Edwards (1969) found that their reinforcement procedures reduced white bias in the children and that children whose white bias had been weakened generalized their attitude to people. They showed less of a tendency to describe African Americans negatively and Whites positively. The investigators pointed out, however, that while the change in racial attitudes was statistically significant, it was not substantial. Williams and Edwards emphasized that even though the reinforcement procedure reduced white bias, it did not remove the children's color connotations for black and white. They wrote: "In the typical case, the procedure merely weakened the customary connotations of white as good and black as bad, and left the child with no consistent evaluative response to the colors" (p. 748).

These findings were confirmed in a study reported later (Edwards & Williams, 1970). Most laboratory interventions by other researchers have, in the main, confirmed these major findings by Williams and his colleagues (Hohn, 1973; Parish & Fleetwood, 1975; Parish, Shirazi, & Lambert, 1976): (1) that preschool children tend to evaluate the color black negatively and the color white positively, (2) that reinforcement procedures can reduce bias toward white, and (3) that children can generalize their reduced white bias to African American people.

Spencer and Horowitz (1973), using procedures they adapted from Renninger and Williams (1966), examined the color perception of 24 African American and White children and designed a reinforcement procedure to modify their color connotations and racial attitudes. They found that the African American preschool children were as negative about the color black as were the White preschoolers, that the children generalized color concepts to racial concepts, that social and token reinforcement reduced white bias, and that the effects of the experiment were evident over a two-week period and for some children over a four-week period.

Perceptual Differentiation Studies

In a series of interesting and innovative studies, Katz and her colleagues (P. A. Katz, 1973; P. A. Katz, Sohn, & Zalk, 1975; P. A. Katz & Zalk, 1978) examined the perceptual concomitants of racial attitudes in young children. She predicted that preschool children would have more difficulty differentiating the faces of out-group individuals than the faces of individuals who were members of their own racial groups (P. A. Katz, 1973). She tested this prediction using a sample of 192 African American and White preschool children who lived in New York City. Katz's prediction was confirmed; she concluded that "racial labels may increase the perceptual similarity of faces of another group" (P. A. Katz, 1973, p. 298).

Katz reasoned that if children could be taught to perceptually differentiate minority-group faces, racial prejudice would be reduced. Katz and Zalk (1978) investigated the effect of teaching children to differentiate minority-group faces in an important study in which they also examined the effects of three other interventions: increased positive racial contact, vicarious interracial contact, and reinforcement of the color black. The researchers examined the effects of these interventions on second- and fifth-grade White students who were high in prejudice. The children were randomly assigned to one of the four experimental treatment groups.

The experimental interventions are described here. In the racial contact situation, two African American and two White children worked together to complete a jigsaw puzzle as fast as they could in order to win a prize. Each of the experimental interventions lasted for 15 minutes in order to control for time. The children in the vicarious contact situation listened to a story with slides that described an African American boy (for the males) or girl (for the females) who was heroic. In one of the experimental conditions for the stimulus predifferentiation groups, the children were shown four slides of the same model that varied along several dimensions. In the other condition, they observed African American faces. This intervention taught the children to differentiate minority-group faces. The children participated in several tasks in the reinforcement condition. In one of them, they were shown 10 black and 10 white animal pictures. When they chose a black animal, they were reinforced with marbles that could be exchanged for prizes.

The investigators found that each of the interventions resulted in a short-term reduction of prejudice on the combined attitude measures used in the study. The most effective interventions for reducing prejudice were the vicarious contact and the perceptual differentiation conditions. The children's racial attitudes were measured two weeks after the experiment and again four to six months later. The experimental gains were reduced over time, but some were maintained. The vicarious contact and perceptual differentiation groups were the most effective interventions for inducing long-term effects.

Curriculum Interventions

Since the 1940s, a number of curriculum intervention studies have been conducted to determine the effects of teaching units and lessons, multiethnic materials, role playing, and other kinds of simulated experiences on the racial attitudes and perceptions of students.

One of the earliest studies was conducted by Trager and Yarrow (1952), who examined the effects of a curriculum intervention on the racial attitudes of children in the first and second grades. In one experimental condition, the children experienced a democratic curriculum; in the other, nondemocratic values were taught and perpetuated. No experimental condition was created in the control group. The democratic curriculum had a positive effect on the attitudes of both the students and teachers.

White second-grade children developed more positive racial attitudes after using multiethnic readers in a study conducted by Litcher and Johnson (1969). However, when Litcher, Johnson, and Ryan (1973) replicated this study using photographs instead of readers, the children's racial attitudes were not significantly changed. The investigators stated that the shorter length of the later study (one month compared to four), as well as the different racial compositions of the two communities in which the studies were conducted, may help to explain why no significant effects were produced on the children's racial attitudes in the second study. The community in which the second study was conducted had a much higher percentage of African American residents than did the community in which the first was conducted.

A longitudinal evaluation of the television program "Sesame Street" by Bogatz and Ball (1971) supports the postulate that multiethnic simulated materials and interventions can have a positive effect on the racial attitudes of young children. These investigators found that children who had watched the program for long periods had more positive racial attitudes toward out-groups than did children who had watched the show for shorter periods.

The effects of a simulation on the racial attitudes of third-grade children was examined by Weiner and Wright (1973). They divided a class into orange and green people, and the children wore colored armbands that designated their group status. On one day of the intervention the students who wore orange armbands experienced discrimination; on the other day, the children who wrote green armbands were the victims. On the third day and again two weeks later, the children expressed less prejudiced beliefs and attitudes.

The effects of multiethnic social studies materials and related experiences on the racial attitudes of African American 4-year-old children were examined by Yawkey and Blackwell (1974). The children were divided into three groups. The students in Group 1 read and discussed the materials. The Group 2 students read and discussed the materials and also took a related field trip. The students in Group 3 experienced the traditional preschool curriculum. The interventions in Groups 1 and 2 had a significant, positive effect on the students' racial attitudes toward African American and Whites.

Cooperative Learning and Interracial Contact

Since 1970, a group of investigators has conducted an impressive body of research on the effects of cooperative learning groups and activities on students' racial attitudes, friendship choices, and achievement. Much of this research has been conducted as well as reviewed by investigators such as Aronson and his colleagues (Aronson & Bridgeman, 1979; Aronson & Gonzalez, 1988), Cohen (E. G. Cohen, 1972, 1986; E. G. Cohen & Roper, 1972), Johnson and Johnson (1981, 1991), and Slavin (1979, 1983, 1985). Most of this research has been conducted using elementary and high school students as subjects, rather than kindergarten and primary-grade students (Slavin, 1983, 1985).

The research on cooperative learning and interracial contact conducted since 1970 has been based on the theory of intergroup relations developed by Allport (1954). Allport stated that prejudice would be reduced if the intergroup situation was cooperative rather than competitive, if group members pursued common goals, if group members had equal status, if group members got to know each other as individuals, and if the contact had institutional support and was sanctioned by authorities.

The research accumulated since 1970 lends considerable support to the postulate that if the conditions stated by Allport are present, cooperative interracial contact situations in schools have positive effects on both student interracial behavior and student academic achievement (Aronson & Gonzalez,

1988; Slavin, 1979, 1983). In his review of 19 studies of the effects of cooperative learning methods, Slavin (1985) found that 16 had positive effects on interracial friendships.

Most of this research supports these postulates: (1) that students of color and White students have a greater tendency to make cross-racial friendship choices after they have participated in interracial learning teams such as the jigsaw (Aronson & Bridgeman, 1979) and the Student Teams–Achievement Divisions (STAD) (Slavin, 1979); (2) that the academic achievement of students of color such as African Americans and Mexican Americans is increased when cooperative learning activities are used; and (3) that the academic achievement of White students remains about the same in both cooperative and competitive learning situations (Aronson & Gonzalez, 1988). Investigators have also found that cooperative learning methods have increased student motivation and self-esteem (Slavin, 1985) and have helped students to develop empathy (Aronson & Bridgeman, 1979).

An essential characteristic of effective cooperative learning groups and methods is that the students experience equal-status contact (Allport, 1954). E. G. Cohen (1972) has pointed out that both African American and White students may expect and attribute higher status to Whites in an initial interracial contact situation that may perpetuate White dominance. E. G. Cohen and Roper (1972) designed an intervention to change this expectation. They taught African American children to build transistor radios and to teach this skill to others. The African American children taught the White children to build the radios after the children watched a videotape showing the African American children building radios. When interracial work groups were structured, only those in which the African American children had taught the White students to build radios experienced equal status. The White children dominated in the other groups. The research by E. G. Cohen and Roper (1972) indicates that equal status between groups in interracial situations has to be constructed rather than assumed.

Summary

The four types of intervention studies reviewed above lend considerable support to the postulate that the racial attitudes and interracial behavior of students can be changed by well-conceptualized and well-planned interventions. As P. A. Katz (1976) has pointed out, the intervention research on children is much more hopeful than the intervention research on adults; the latter indicates that it is much more difficult to change adult racial attitudes and behaviors because they are well crystallized and tenacious (Stephan, 1985). This research indicates that early childhood educators have the best opportunity to positively influence the racial and ethnic attitudes of children. It becomes increasingly difficult to influence the attitudes of children as they grow older and move through the grades.

The laboratory reinforcement studies indicate that the bias that young children have toward the color white can be reduced by interventions that reinforce the color black. Furthermore, when white bias in young children is reduced, this reduction of bias is generalized to people. P. A. Katz (1973, 1982) and her colleagues (P. A. Katz & Zalk, 1978) have established the fact that it is more difficult for children to differentiate the faces of out-group individuals than it is for them to differentiate the faces of individuals who are members of their own racial groups. Interventions can help children differentiate the faces of out-group individuals and also reduce prejudice toward out-groups.

A variety of curriculum interventions can be used to help students develop more positive racial attitudes and perceptions, including multicultural materials, vicarious experiences, role playing, and simulations. The most famous race-related curriculum intervention is the one undertaken by Jane Elliott, a third-grade teacher in Riceville, Iowa, who discriminated against brown-eyed children the first day and blue-eyed children the next. Elliot's intervention is described in a book (Peters, 1987) as well as in two video presentations, *The Eye of the Storm* and *A Class Divided.* Research also indicates that cooperative learning activities and experiences, if they have the characteristics identified by Allport (1954), can help students to develop more friendships across racial groups. Cooperative learning activities can also help students of color, such as African Americans and Mexican Americans, to increase their academic achievement. However, some research indicates that cooperative learning activities do not have a measurable effect on the academic achievement of White mainstream students (Aronson & Gonzalez, 1988).

IMPLICATIONS FOR PRACTICE: THE NEED FOR TOTAL SCHOOL REFORM

Research over the last 60 years has established the fact that young children have accurate knowledge about racial differences and the evaluations that society makes of different racial and ethnic groups (Aboud, 1987; Clark & Clark, 1939; Lasker, 1929; Milner, 1983). Researchers have also established that by the age of 4 most White children have developed strong in-group preferences and negative attitudes toward other racial groups (Aboud, 1987; Milner, 1983). Research is less clear about the extent to which African American and Mexican American children make in-group preferences. What is clear, however, is that many of them make more out-group than in-group preferences and that others make biracial choices because of the ways in which they are socialized.

The research reviewed in this chapter indicates that educators can help students to develop more positive racial attitudes and behaviors (defined here as biracial choices) by implementing well-planned and well-conceptualized curricular interventions. Major goals of these interventions should be to help students of all racial, ethnic, and cultural groups to develop more positive connotations for brown and other nonwhite colors; to have positive vicarious experiences with people from a variety of racial and ethnic groups; to learn to differentiate the faces of individuals from different racial and ethnic groups; and, where possible, to have positive cross-racial interactions with children from different ethnic groups that are characterized by cooperation, equal status, and shared goals, and that are sanctioned by the teacher and the school culture.

To implement the principles derived from the research reviewed in this chapter, *multicultural education* must be implemented, defined here as a restructuring and transformation of the total school environment so that it reflects the racial and cultural diversity within U.S. society and helps children from diverse groups to experience educational equality (Banks, 1988b, 1991b; Banks & Banks, 1989). To successfully implement multicultural education, the total school must be conceptualized as a unit and significant changes must be made in each of its major variables, such as the values and attitudes of the school staff, the curriculum and teaching materials, assessment and testing procedures, teaching and motivational styles, and the values and norms sanctioned and perpetuated by the school. A number of useful resources are available to help practitioners implement multicultural education for young children, which is the best time for it to begin (Banks, 1991b; Derman-Sparks & the A.B.C. Task Force, 1989; Kendall, 1983; Ramsey, 1987; Saracho & Spodek, 1983).

The Importance of the Teacher

The teacher is a key variable in successfully implementing multicultural education and in helping students to develop democratic racial attitudes and behaviors. Teachers are human beings who bring their cultural perspectives, values, hopes, and dreams to the classroom. The teacher's values and behaviors strongly influence the views, conceptions, and behaviors of students. The teacher's values and perspectives also mediate and interact with what they teach and influence the ways that messages are communicated and perceived by students. Teachers who makes strong in-group preferences and believe that white is more beautiful than brown or that Whites have been the main contributors to American culture and civilization will, whether they intend to or not, convey these attitudes and beliefs to students. Consequently, to implement an effective program of multicultural education, teacher education is essential because most American teachers have internalized many of the

Eurocentric values and attitudes that young children often exemplified in the research reviewed in this chapter (Gay, 1986).

Teacher educators should help classroom teachers attain the knowledge, attitudes, and skills they need to function effectively in the multicultural class-room of the twenty-first century (Banks, 1988b, 1991b; Gay, 1986). This should be done because we need to create a more caring nation, as well as because of the demographic changes that are taking place in U.S. society. About 46% of the nation's school-age youth will be students of color by 2020 (Pallas, Natriello, & McDill, 1989). The increasing racial, ethnic, and cultural diversity in the nation is presenting new challenges as well as opportunities. If the United States does not become a more culturally sensitive society in which citizens from different racial and cultural groups can live and work in harmony, its survival as a strong and democratic nation will be imperiled. The research described in this chapter provides educators hope as well as spe-cific guidelines for the decisive action needed to transform the total school culture. Transformation of the total school is essential in order to create citi-zens who have the multicultural literacy, perspectives, and cross-cultural competencies needed to function effectively in the twenty-first century.

PART IV

Educating Teachers, Leaders, and Citizens

Teachers, as well as other educators and leaders, must play an important role in educating students from diverse groups to become effective citizens in a democratic society. To become thoughtful and active citizens, students must experience democracy in classrooms and in schools. Action speaks much more cogently than words. Consequently, how teachers respond to marginalized students in the classroom will to a great extent determine whether they will experience democracy or oppression in classrooms and schools.

To create democratic schools for students from diverse racial, ethnic, and cultural groups, teachers must examine their cultural assumptions and attitudes, their behaviors, the knowledge and paradigms on which their pedagogy is based, and the subject-matter knowledge they teach. They must also teach students how to examine the knowledge embedded in the school curriculum.

Chapters 9 and 10 examine issues related to educating teachers, leaders, and scholars in ways that will enable them to effectively participate in the project to educate reflective and transformative citizens in a democratic, pluralistic society. Chapter 11 describes the goals of citizenship education in a pluralistic nation-state.

9

TEACHING MULTICULTURAL LITERACY TO TEACHERS

The drastic decline in the percentage of teachers of color that is projected for the turn of the century and that is already occurring has been well documented (R. Wilson & Melendez, 1987). Teachers of color made up 12.5% of the nation's teachers in 1980. If current trends continue, they will make up about 5% of the nation's teachers by 2000. The percentage of students of color in the nation's schools is rapidly increasing as the percentage of teachers of color is declining precipitously. About 46% of the nation's school-age youths (ages 0 to 18) will be students of color by 2020 (Pallas, Natriello, & McDill, 1989). Students of color constitute the majority of students today in 25 of the nation's 50 largest school districts. These important demographic trends have important implications for the recruitment, education, and retention of students in teacher education programs.

An important implication of the demographic changes described above is that more students of color should be recruited for teacher education programs. This important aspect of the problem has received deserved attention in the educational literature. However, an aspect of the problem that merits more attention is the declining number of students of color who are enrolling in colleges and universities, and the need for recruitment efforts to focus more generally on increasing the number of students of color who enter and complete college. At all levels of higher education, African American enrollment was considerably lower during the 1984–85 academic year than during the 1980–81 academic year (R. Wilson & Melendez, 1987).

The larger the pool of college students of color, the greater are the chances of increasing the percentage of them who enter teacher education programs. Consequently, a strategy is needed to increase the pool of students of color who enter and complete college. Such efforts need to start as early as junior high school.

Another important aspect of the problem has received insufficient attention in the educational literature: the need to help all teachers—especially

White mainstream teachers—acquire the attitudes, skills, and knowledge needed to work effectively with students of color. Even if we are successful in increasing the percentage of teachers of color from the projected 5% in 2000 to 15%, 85% of the nation's teachers will still be White, mainstream, and largely female. Because of the changing characteristics of the nation's student population, a large percentage of teachers will be working with students who differ from them racially, culturally, and in social-class status. An effective teacher education policy for the twenty-first century must include as a major focus the education of all teachers—including teachers of color—in ways that will help them to acquire the knowledge, skills, and attitudes needed to work effectively with students from diverse racial, ethnic, and social-class groups.

An effective teacher education program should include both preservice and inservice components. A strong inservice component is especially important, because many teachers will remain in the classroom as their student population changes racially, ethnically, culturally, and in social-class status. Without inservice education, these teachers are likely to develop negative attitudes and lower expectations as the characteristics of their students change.

Multicultural education courses and experiences are an essential component of such a teacher education program. In this chapter, I identify and describe some of the major goals and strategies that I use in an ethnic studies course for preservice and inservice teachers.

KNOWLEDGE GOALS OF THE COURSE

To function effectively in multicultural classrooms, teachers need at least three major kinds of knowledge: (1) *social science knowledge* about the nature of their societies and about the diverse cultural and ethnic groups that make up their societies; (2) *pedagogical knowledge* to help them make effective instructional decisions and become skillful in the classroom; and (3) *subject-matter content knowledge*. My course is designed to help teachers acquire social science knowledge about the nature of cultural and ethnic diversity in U.S. society and pedagogical knowledge about ways to integrate ethnic content into the curriculum. Some attention is also devoted to pedagogical knowledge related to the learning styles and characteristics of students from diverse ethnic and cultural groups and the teaching implications of this knowledge. The course does not attempt to help students to acquire subject-matter content knowledge about their disciplines, since this is the major aim of courses they have already taken.

SOCIAL SCIENCE KNOWLEDGE
ABOUT DIVERSITY IN U.S. SOCIETY

Traditionally, social science knowledge has been an important component of the teacher education curriculum in most Western societies (Alexander, Craft, & Lynch, 1984). Most teachers are required to take courses that deal with the historical, sociological, and political aspects of their societies and nation-states. However, most of this knowledge has several characteristics that prevent teacher education students from attaining the insights, understandings, and skills needed to function successfully in culturally diverse classrooms.

We can think of bodies of knowledge, such as paradigms and theories (Kuhn, 1970; Merton, 1968; Popkewitz, 1984), as consisting of several components (e.g., assumptions and values, modes of inquiry or processes, and products). The dominant trend in teacher education programs is to teach students the products of knowledge, devoting scant attention to the assumptions and values that undergird the knowledge and making little effort to engage students in a process that involves formulating and attaining knowledge.

Because teacher education students attain most of their knowledge without analyzing its assumptions and values or engaging in the process of constructing knowledge themselves, they often leave teacher education programs with many misconceptions about culturally and racially different groups and with conceptions about their national history and culture that are incomplete, misleading, and chauvinistic. Consequently, the knowledge that many teachers bring to the classroom contributes to the mystification rather than to the clarification of social, historical, and political realities. This knowledge also perpetuates inequality and victimization rather than contributes to justice and liberation.

In order to educate teachers so that they will convey images, perspectives, and points of view that will demystify social realities and promote cultural freedom and empowerment, we must radically change the way in which they acquire knowledge. We must engage them in a process of attaining knowledge in which they are required to analyze conflicting paradigms and explanations and to critically analyze the values and assumptions of different paradigms and theories. Teacher education students must also be given the opportunity to construct concepts, generalizations, and theories so that they can develop a sophisticated appreciation for the nature and limitations of knowledge and understand the extent to which knowledge reflects the social and cultural context in which it is formulated.

Participating in processes in which they formulate and construct various knowledge forms will also help teacher education students understand how various groups in society who formulate, shape, and disseminate knowledge often structure and disseminate knowledge that supports their interests and legitimizes their power. This knowledge often justifies the status quo and makes victimized and powerless groups politically passive and content with their deprived status. If teachers are to become agents of liberation and change they need to understand how knowledge is often used to keep deprived groups victimized (Banks, 1984).

Understanding Knowledge as a Social Construction

Films, videotapes, and documents that describe events from different perspectives are among the techniques that I use to help my students understand knowledge as a social construction and understand how knowledge reflects the experiences, struggles, hopes, and dreams of a people. One of the most powerful experiences for my students is the viewing of the film *How the West Was Won . . . and Honor Lost, Part I.* Narrated by Marlon Brando, the film documents how the lands of the Indians were acquired by the White settlers through broken treaties, cultural misunderstandings, and deceit. It also describes, in poignant detail, how the Indians were forced to leave their lands and to settle in Indian Territory.

The questions that the students are asked to discuss in groups of five after seeing the film are designed to help them view the removal of the Indians from a perspective different from the one that is institutionalized in the popular culture as well as to help them analyze and clarify their feelings about the events depicted in the film. They are also asked a question that helps them develop pedagogical skills and to consider how and why they might use the film in their own teaching.

The use of this film to attain multiple but highly interrelated goals and objectives illustrates a salient characteristic of my course. Because the goals of the course are highly interrelated, I always consider ways in which a particular experience, such as the viewing of a film or videotape, can help the students develop knowledge and skills related to several major objectives of the course. Most adults have strong opinions, attitudes, and beliefs about racial and ethnic groups. Consequently, when students view a film such as *How the West Was Won . . . and Honor Lost*, they can learn new perspectives about historical events as well as examine their racial and ethnic attitudes related to these events.

Many students state that the events in the film are presented from an Indian perspective. Other students point out that the perspective is a White liberal one and that an Indian perspective would differ in subtle but important ways. The students also discuss how the perspective presented in the film is different from the ones about Indian–White relationships that they have learned from the popular culture, particularly from Western movies on television. In our class discussion, we do not try to resolve the question of the perspective from which the film is presented. Rather, the goal is attained when the students realize that the perspective on the removal of Indians presented in this film differs in significant ways from the ones that they learned in school and from the popular culture.

Some of the most interesting comments made by the students are given in response to this question: How did the film make you feel? Frequently appearing words are *angry*, *ashamed*, and *sad*. The students state that they are angry because the view of Indian–White relationships described in the film has been hidden from them until now. They state that they feel like they have been betrayed by the educational system. The students who are ashamed and sad state that they have these feelings because of the roles their White ancestors played in the victimization of American Indians. In our follow-up discussion of their feelings, I point out to the students that there were also Whites who participated in the elimination of racism and discrimination, such as John Brown, Helen Hunt Jackson, and William Lloyd Garrison. I also point out that their personal responsibility is to help eliminate racism and discrimination in society today rather than feel guilty about what happened in the past.

We also discuss how the students might handle strong emotions, such as anger and shame, that will be expressed by both their students of color and their White students when they teach ethnic content in their own classes. Among the points that we make is that we should help students to understand that their emotions are valid, that it is okay to express them in the classroom, and that students should be helped to understand that powerful emotions are an essential part of studying about content related to racial and ethnic diversity in U.S. society. The students discuss these questions in small groups after viewing *How the West Was Won . . . and Honor Lost:*

1. From whose perspective are the events presented?
2. What are other possible perspectives and points of view on the same events?
3. How did the film make you feel?
4. Would you use this film in your teaching? If so, why and how? If not, why not?

Multicultural Education Paradigms

I introduce the concept of *paradigms*, or systems of explanation (Kuhn, 1970), in my course to help the students better understand the nature of knowledge, the assumptions that underlie different kinds of knowledge, and the teaching implications of different paradigms.

We can identify paradigms, theories, and knowledge claims that perpetuate inequality and that most teachers learned during their training programs. These forms of knowledge make it difficult for teachers to become agents of liberation and social change. I describe 10 paradigms that are common in the multicultural education literature in another publication (Banks, 1988b). The *genetic* and *cultural deprivation* paradigms are two theoretical systems that are commonly found in the literature on the education of ethnic groups. Both of these paradigms promote educational inequality because they provide educators with easy alibis for not teaching students of color and lower-class students basic academic skills. Using either of these paradigms, educators can "blame the victims" for their academic failures. The cultural deprivation paradigm assumes that students of color and low-income students do not achieve well in school because of the pathologies in their family and community cultures. The genetic paradigm assumes that low-income students and students of color do not achieve well in school because of their inferior genetic characteristics.

The genetic paradigm, which is strongly entrenched in the U.S. educational establishment, is based on a limited and outmoded conception of human intelligence. Alternative paradigms, such as the concept of *multiple intelligences* (Gardner, 1983), have emerged and challenged the genetic paradigm in recent years. However, most educational practitioners either reject or are unaware of these newer paradigms and continue to hold traditional and highly restricted notions of human intelligence (Mercer, 1989). As Jeannie Oakes (1985) documents in her important book, *Keeping Track*, lower-class students and students of color are often victimized by these outmoded conceptions of human intelligence because they are placed in lower academic tracks where they receive an inferior education from teachers who believe they do not have the ability to learn.

My students are required to analyze a range of paradigms and theories that give conflicting explanations of the nature of their societies. Consequently, they gain new perspectives on their own cultures as well as those of their students. They are also given opportunities to engage in processes that will enable them to formulate concepts, generalizations, and theories about the social, economic, and political conditions in the United States and the world. As they analyze and formulate various theories and paradigms, they are asked to determine which perpetuate the status quo and which can best be used to help students of color attain educational equality and cultural freedom.

Teacher education students need to understand how different concepts, paradigms, and theories lead to different educational policies and practices. The *racism, radical,* and *cultural difference* paradigms give students very different ways of interpreting the experiences of ethnic groups from those given by the genetic and cultural deprivation paradigms. These paradigms also lead to very different kinds of educational policies and practices. These three paradigms assume that the low academic achievement of poor students and students of color can, to a large extent, be explained by structural inequality, class stratification, and institutionalized racism. The racism, radical, and cultural difference paradigms legitimize significant social change; the genetic and cultural deprivation paradigms justify the status quo.

Cultural Identity and Values

Teachers are human beings who bring their cultural perspectives, values, hopes, and dreams to the classroom. They also bring their prejudices, stereotypes, and misconceptions. Teachers' values and perspectives mediate and interact with what they teach and influence the way that their messages are communicated to and perceived by their students. A teacher who believes that Christopher Columbus "discovered" America and one who believes that Columbus came to America when it was peopled by groups with rich and diverse cultures will send different messages to their students when the European exploration of America is studied.

Because the teacher mediates the messages and symbols communicated to the students through the curriculum, it is important for teachers to come to grips with their own personal and cultural values and identities in order for them to help students from diverse racial, ethnic, and cultural groups develop clarified cultural identities and relate positively to one another. I am hypothesizing that self-clarification is a prerequisite to dealing effectively with and relating positively to outside ethnic and cultural groups. An Anglo American teacher who is confused about his or her cultural identity and who has a nonreflective conception of the ways in which Anglo American culture relates to other groups in the United States will have a very difficult time relating positively to ethnic groups such as African Americans and Mexican Americans.

Effective teacher education courses and programs should help pre- and inservice teachers explore and clarify their own ethnic and cultural identities and develop more positive attitudes toward other racial, ethnic, and cultural groups. To do this, courses and programs must recognize and reflect the complex ethnic and cultural identities and characteristics of the individuals in teacher education programs. Teachers should also learn how to facilitate the identity quests among students and help them to become effective and able participants in the common civic culture.

To develop a teacher education curriculum that reflects the myriad and emerging ethnic and cultural identities among teachers, we must make some attempt to identify them and to describe their curricular and teaching implications. A typology that attempts to outline the stages of the development of

ethnic and cultural identity among individuals is described in another publication (Banks, 1988b). The typology, an ideal-type construct in the Weberian
sense, constitutes a set of hypotheses that are based on the existing and
emerging theory and research and on the author's study of ethnic and cultural behavior. The typology suggests preliminary guidelines for teaching
about ethnic and cultural diversity in the common schools and colleges and
for helping teachers function effectively at increasingly higher stages of ethnic
and cultural development. The typology is summarized in Figure 9.1. In the
next section of this chapter, I describe the ways in which I help my students
develop a better understanding of their cultural and ethnic identities and
experiences and develop higher stages of ethnic and cultural development.

Writing a Family History

I use a variety of techniques and strategies to help my students, most of
whom have European American backgrounds, to better understand their own
cultural experiences, to develop greater insights into other cultures, and to
relate more positively to them. During the first unit of the course, I ask the
students to read autobiographical accounts that describe the anguish of being
a White ethnic in American society, such as "Stepchild of America: Growing
Up Polish" by Thomas Napierkowski (1976) and "The Education of Harriet
Pawlowska" by Harriet Pawlowska (1976).

After the students have read the autobiographical accounts by European
Americans, they listen to an audiotape by Alex Haley (1977) in which he
describes his search for his roots, which took him to Africa and back to
America. I juxtapose autobiographical writings by European Americans with
the audiotape by Haley to help the students to see how the experiences of
America's diverse ethnic groups have been both similar and different. The
reading of the autobiographical accounts, the listening to the tape by Haley,
and the viewing of a filmstrip on the saga of a Jewish American family are
designed to help students acquire the knowledge, motivation, and insights
needed to prepare the family history that each student writes during the first
part of the course.

The students are given a guide for preparing a family history, which is
described by Cortés, Metcalf, and Hawke (1976). Called "What Is My Ethnic
Background?", the guide requires the students to make a family tree of their
ancestors and to conduct interviews with relatives. I encourage the students
to use the guide freely and to omit steps they do not find helpful in writing
their reports. Each student is required to write his or her family history in
narrative form, to share it with a small group in the class, and to submit it to
me for evaluation. The writing of their family histories is a very meaningful
and powerful assignment for the students. One Anglo American student said

Figure 9.1 The Stages of Ethnicity: A Typology

Stage 1:
Ethnic
Psychological
Captivity

The individual internalizes the negative societal beliefs about his or her ethnic group.

Stage 2:
Ethnic
Encapsulation

The individual is ethnocentric and practices ethnic separatism.

Stage 3:
Ethnic Identity
Clarification

The individual accepts self and has clarified attitudes toward his or her own ethnic group.

Stage 4:
Biethnicity

The individual has the attitudes, skills, and commitment needed to participate both within his or her own ethnic group and within another ethnic culture.

Stage 5:
Multiethnicity
and
Reflective
Nationalism

The individual has reflective ethnic and national identifications and the skills, attitudes, and commitment needed to function within a range of ethnic and cultural groups within his or her nation.

Stage 6:
Globalism and
Global
Competency

The individual has reflective and positive ethnic, national, and global identifications and the knowledge, skills, and commitment needed to function within cultures throughout his or her nation and world.

Reprinted with permission from J. A. Banks, *Multiethnic education: Theory and practice* (3rd ed.), Boston: Allyn & Bacon, 1994, p. 60.

to me shortly after completing her family history: "I am very glad that ethnic studies now includes Whites!" Once my students have explored their own cultural and ethnic roots, they are then able to study the cultures of other ethnic groups in the United States—such as African Americans and Mexican Americans—not only with more empathy but also with more understanding and enthusiasm.

The students also read *Balm in Gilead: Journey of A Healer*, Sara Lawrence Lightfoot's (1988) powerful and moving biography of her mother, one of the nation's first African American child psychiatrists. To enable the students to gain historical knowledge about the various racial and ethnic groups in the United States, they read the historical chapters in my book, *Teaching Strategies for Ethnic Studies* (Banks, 1991b).

Helping students to better understand their own cultural experiences and to develop more clarified cultural and ethnic identifications is only the first step in helping them to better understand and relate to other ethnic and racial groups. They also need experiences that will enable them to learn about the values and attitudes they hold toward other ethnic and cultural groups, to clarify and analyze their values, to reflect on the consequences of their values and attitudes, to consider alternative attitudes and values, and to personally confront some of their latent values and attitudes toward other groups and races.

Case Studies and Role Playing

The goals described above are attained by having students work with open-ended case studies that present real-life dilemmas and problems both in discussion groups and in role-playing situations. They role-play or formulate several different solutions to a problem and discuss the possible consequences of each possible solution. Preservice students who are observing or working in schools and inservice students can be asked to write case studies that describe intergroup problems they have observed or heard described in their schools.

Students can also be asked to carefully observe students from different ethnic and racial groups in the classroom and on the playground and to describe examples of problems in intergroup relations that warrant teacher intervention. These types of behavioral samples can be used as case studies. The students can discuss what possible actions teachers could take to help resolve the problems. Students need to see and study examples of effective case studies before they are asked to write them. Grambs (1968) describes an open-ended case, *Junior Prom*, that I use effectively to help my students think about intergroup relations problems in schools, analyze their values related to ethnic stereotyping and insensitivity, and discuss similar intergroup problems in their own schools.

In *Junior Prom*, the students' teacher and adviser for the prom, Mrs. Richardson, talks with three of the students who played a leading role in planning the prom about a problem the principal has brought to her attention. The theme for the prom is a fiesta. The poster for the prom shows Mexicans with sombreros over their faces sleeping under a cactus. Mrs. Richardson tells the students that the Mexican American students feel that the poster is offensive and asks them what can be done to solve the problem. The students do not perceive a problem. They react angrily to Mrs. Richardson's observations. They argue that they should not let a few students in the school dictate the theme for the prom or the design for the poster. Besides, they point out, they cannot change the theme or the poster because they have spent all of the money budgeted for the prom.

I give this case study to my class and ask groups of four students to role-play a solution to it and to discuss whether their solution—if one is attained—is realistic and what might be its possible consequences. The students also discuss the values of Mrs. Richardson, Mr. Perkins (the principal), and the students toward ethnic and racial differences. I also ask them to identify the *main problem* in the case. They usually conclude, after I have used probing questions during an in-depth discussion, that the main problem is the negative racial attitudes and ethnic insensitivity that are pervasive in the community and the school.

The racial attitudes of Mr. Perkins and Mrs. Richardson are little different from those of the students. My students usually think that Mr. Perkins is merely acting on the problem because he has received complaints from Mexican American students and perhaps from a few parents. If Mr. Perkins and Mrs. Richardson had been sensitive to the racial and ethnic differences in their school and community, they would have established a school environment in which an insensitive poster would most likely not have been developed by the students. The prom incident is symptomatic of more basic race relations problems within the school. Consequently, major curricular reform and teacher inservice training is needed to deal with the main problem exemplified in *Junior Prom*.

Pedagogical Knowledge and Skills

It is necessary, but not sufficient, for teachers to master social science knowledge about their societies and to develop clarified cultural identifications and positive racial attitudes. They also need to master pedagogical knowledge and skills that will enable them to make effective instructional decisions, to accurately diagnose the learning problems of students from diverse groups, to formulate teaching strategies that motivate them, and to create a classroom environment that respects the culture of each child and helps students from diverse groups to interact positively.

Teachers who have strong social science knowledge, clarified cultural identifications, and positive racial attitudes will not be successful in the multicultural classroom unless they also have pedagogical knowledge and skills. Teachers in multicultural societies need: (1) knowledge about the unique cultural characteristics and learning styles of students from diverse cultural groups and the skills to teach these students successfully (Banks, 1988a); (2) knowledge about the nature of prejudice, as well as strategies that can be used to reduce prejudice among students (Banks, 1991a); and (3) general knowledge and skills about teaching that can be adapted to meet the specific needs of students from diverse racial, ethnic, and cultural groups.

The knowledge and skills described above are taught in the ethnic studies course described in this chapter as well as in a required course that I team teach that focuses on race, class, gender, and exceptionality. Each professor in the teacher education program is also encouraged to infuse content related to ethnic, cultural, and gender diversity into his or her course, such as methods courses in reading, the language arts, the social studies, science, and mathematics. Our faculty believes that students need to study content related to cultural and ethnic diversity in specialized courses in ethnic studies and multicultural education as well as across the teacher education curriculum if they are to be prepared to function effectively in the diverse classrooms of the next century.

10

MULTICULTURAL EDUCATION: GOALS FOR THE TWENTY-FIRST CENTURY

Multicultural education is moving down the road toward academic legitimacy and institutionalization. Signs of health and vitality are the establishment of required multicultural teacher education courses in a large number of colleges and universities; the proliferation of multicultural education textbooks, scholarly books, and articles; the brisk sales of several leading textbooks; the establishment of a national organization, the National Association of Multicultural Education (NAME) and its magazine, *Multicultural Education*; and the publication of the first *Handbook of Research on Multicultural Education* (Banks & Banks, 1995b). The *Handbook* brings together in one volume the major scholarship, research, and theory that has developed since the field evolved in the 1970s.

CHALLENGES TO MULTICULTURAL EDUCATION IN THE NEXT CENTURY

These significant markers of the development of multicultural education, a nascent and practical field, should not prevent us from recognizing and conceptualizing ways to deal with the challenges the field faces as it enters the twenty-first century. We should also view the progress and challenges to the field within a historical context. To provide such a context, I will briefly discuss the historical development of anthropology and sociology. Space does not permit a discussion of the significant ways in which academic disciplines such as anthropology and sociology and fields such as multicultural education, which are grounded in practice, differ.

During the late nineteenth and early twentieth centuries, the social science disciplines such as anthropology and sociology were in a nascent phase and had to struggle to attain academic legitimacy and institutionalization. At that time, the physical and natural sciences reigned supreme in the colleges and universities. The new social sciences tried to gain legitimacy by attempting to adapt and incorporate the aims and methods of the physical and natural sciences. In fact, a number of early pioneers in these disciplines, such as anthropologist Franz Boas and sociologist Lester Frank Ward, had received their advanced degrees and training in the natural and physical sciences.

The Legitimization and Institutionalization of Anthropology and Sociology

The social sciences, such as anthropology and sociology, survived and eventually gained academic legitimacy. They also became institutionalized as departments in the nation's leading research universities. Several factors contributed to their success and implementation. One of the most important was the strong academic leadership provided by such scholars as Franz Boas (United States) and Bronislaw Malinowski (United Kingdom) in anthropology and William G. Sumner and Lester Frank Ward in sociology. The sociologists of the "Chicago School" of sociology at the University of Chicago also greatly enhanced the academic status of sociology in the years after Sumner and Ward published their seminal works (Bulmer, 1984). William I. Thomas and Robert E. Park published highly influential works at Chicago during the second decade of this century.

The academic leadership provided by scholars such as Boas, Malinowski, Thomas, and Park included the development of paradigms, concepts, and theories that grew out of empirical research in field settings conducted by themselves, their students, and scholars they heavily influenced. The pioneering empirical and theoretical work done by these early leaders in anthropology and sociology was a decisive factor in building these two disciplines. Landmark publications that contributed to the growth and legitimacy of anthropology included *The Mind of Primitive Man* by Boas in 1911 and *Argonauts of the Western Pacific* by Malinowski in 1922. Landmark publications in sociology included *Dynamic Sociology* by Ward in 1883, *Folkways* by Sumner in 1907, *The Polish Peasant in Europe and America* by Thomas and Znaniecki in 1918–1920, and *Introduction to the Science of Sociology* by Park and Burgess in 1921.

The commitment by the early scholars in anthropology and sociology to empirical research and to theory building was the most important factor that led to the academic legitimacy and institutionalization of these disciplines on college and university campuses and in the public imagination.

TWENTY-FIRST CENTURY GOALS

The next several decades will be critical ones for multicultural education as a discipline and field of study and practice. During this period, its fate will be determined. Multicultural education will either attain academic legitimacy and become fully institutionalized within the next several decades or it will fade away like progressive education and intergroup education. I believe that multicultural education will survive and become fully institutionalized in the nation's universities, colleges, and school districts. However, its survival is by no means assured. We can act thoughtfully and decisively in ways that will greatly increase its possibilities for survival and institutionalization. Toward that end, I will offer, for discussion by the profession, what I think ought to be the key goals for multicultural education as it faces the twenty-first century.

The Development of Scholarly Leaders

We need to develop scholarly leaders for the future. Within the next two decades, the torch must be passed to a new generation of scholars and researchers in multicultural education. We need to invest much more of our time, energy, and resources in the development of new scholars for the field.

I am concerned that the identification of future scholars and adequate training and mentoring programs for them are not receiving the attention in the field that is essential for its development. To continue on a path toward institutionalization, leadership within a field must be continuing and consistent over several generations. Anthropology succeeded in part because Boas trained students such as Ruth Benedict and Margaret Mead who continued to develop the field after Boas had completed his most significant works. Yet one of the most important reasons that the intergroup education movement perished is that its leaders, such as Hilda Taba and William Van Til, left the field and pursued other professional interests. Another positive example of the survival of a field because of long, continuing, and consistent leadership is the way in which African American history developed from the early twentieth century to the present. Carter G. Woodson devoted his entire life to research, organizational, and professional work in African American history (Banks, 1992). He also inspired and influenced an entire generation of younger historians—including Rayford Logan, Charles H. Wesley, Benjamin Quarles, and John Hope Franklin—who pursued work in African American history and continued that work beyond Woodson's time.

For a field to survive and prosper, leaders must not only devote a lifetime to its development but must also make sure that younger scholars[1] are trained so that leadership in the field will be strong, consistent, and continuous over many decades. Several generations of scholars must be willing to

---

[1] By *younger scholars* I am not referring to chronological age but rather to new recruits to the field. Ruth Benedict did not receive her doctorate until she was 36, yet she became one of the nation's most widely read and influential anthropologists.

devote lifetimes to a discipline for it to develop and become institutionalized and to gain academic legitimacy. Respect among practitioners tends to follow respect in the academy.

The Primacy of Scholarship Linked with Practice

Scholarship and research, whose aim is to improve practice, must be the field's top priority during the remainder of the 1990s and the first decades of the twenty-first century. The field's quest for academic legitimacy and institutionalization should be an overarching goal that is vigorously and continually pursued. Although it is essential that multicultural education develop its own journals and publications, it is also important for multicultural scholars, researchers, and practitioners to publish frequently in the most respected and influential journals in education. These journals have academic legitimacy, professional authority, and large and influential audiences.

It is going to take several decades for multicultural education to attain the academic legitimacy and respect that it deserves. However, this respect and legitimacy must be earned the hard way—the same way that it was earned by other new fields and disciplines, such as anthropology, sociology, and special education. That is why it is essential that multicultural education invest heavily in the development and mentoring of future scholars who have a deep commitment to and interest in the field.

Since 1980, a number of significant multicultural education articles and papers have been published in highly respected mainstream journals and books. These publications have contributed greatly to the academic legitimization of the field. Among them are Barbara A. Shade's (1982) paper on African American cognitive style in the *Review of Educational Research*; Carl A. Grant and Christine E. Sleeter's (1986) paper on race, class, and gender in the *Review of Educational Research;* the Sleeter and Grant (1987) influential paper describing their multicultural education typology in the *Harvard Educational Review;* and the review of research in the field by James A. Banks (1993e) in the *Review of Research in Education.*

Formulating Standards for the Field

The field needs to discuss the feasibility of developing criteria for determining who can practice in multicultural education, of developing standards and guidelines for multicultural professionals, and of developing minimum standards for practice. A serious problem exists in multicultural education because people with varied—and often sparse—professional education are calling themselves multicultural professionals and are conducting training for business, health care, and educational institutions on a wide and often profitable scale. In their training sessions, these individuals often violate key principles and practices in the field that are derived from theory, research, and wisdom of practice.

It is not uncommon for individuals with varying skills and abilities to proclaim expertise and to practice in nascent fields. In the early years of their discipline, sociologists became deeply concerned because of the wide range of people who called themselves "sociologists." Bernard (1987) writes: "They [sociologists] sought . . . to achieve an identity uncontaminated by quacks who called themselves sociologists. The rapid growth of the study of sociology had created a great shortage of teachers." (p. 197). Lundberg stated in 1929:

> Second-rate and half-trained men have in consequence filled important positions. As a result of the demand for men, sociology has tended to be a sort of happy hunting ground for well-meaning sentimentalists, plausible charlatans, and other worthy persons unwilling or unable to weather the rigorous discipline of real scholarship. (cited in Bernard, 1987, p. 197)

Sociology solved the problem of professional certification and of who could practice in the field by establishing the criterion that trained sociologists must earn a doctorate from a recognized university. The solution for multicultural education will be more difficult because the field is both a research and a practical field. In its early years sociology also had a practical component. However, this component was essentially eliminated during the discipline's quest for legitimacy. Because of the nature of multicultural education, in which practice and the improvement of practice is an integral part of what we are, practice must remain a significant part of the field. However, dialogue ought to take place about the possibility of setting minimum standards for practice in multicultural education.

RESOLVING THE INTEGRATION/SEPARATE COURSE PROBLEM

One of the most difficult issues that multicultural education now faces and will increasingly face in the future is the pressure by mainstream colleagues in teacher education programs to "integrate" the content of multicultural education courses into existing or newly created general teacher education courses. This pressure is likely to mount as the popularity of integrated education courses increases, caused in part by the budget crisis that exists throughout higher education.

To avoid the appearance of mere self-interest, it is essential that we give well-reasoned and thoughtful responses to requests (often disguised demands) to integrate the content of multicultural education courses into existing courses. I strongly believe, however, that the integration model of curriculum reform, if widely implemented nationally, will seriously threaten the existence of multicultural education as a discipline and retard the academic legitimacy and institutionalization of the field.

A total integration model must be resisted on *academic, pragmatic*, and *political* grounds. We should argue for the implementation of a *multicultural education + integration model* (MCE + Integration model), which will ensure that students will learn the key paradigms, concepts, ideologies, and knowledge in multicultural education from committed experts in the field. At the same time, instructors of courses such as foundations, general curriculum, and the subject-matter methods courses will be encouraged and allowed to integrate multicultural content into their courses. If multicultural content is poorly integrated into the general courses (or is not integrated beyond the course outline— both conditions frequently exist), students will still have benefited from the one or two multicultural education courses taught by specialists.

The Academic Justification

I should make my preference for the MCE + Integration model explicit. First, the academic justification for this model: Multicultural education is a distinct interdisciplinary field with a unique set of paradigms, concepts, theories, and skills. It is not highly likely that nonspecialists can adequately teach the specialized content of the field to novice teachers and practitioners. They are likely to be learning the content of the field themselves and may not have much more expertise in multicultural education than their students.

Even if nonspecialists have mastered the academic content of multicultural education, they often have not had adequate opportunities to examine their attitudes, feelings, and beliefs, all important factors in teaching multicultural content. We do not expect or usually permit a nonexpert in reading to teach the content of the readings methods course to novice students or to integrate it into a general methods course that the nonexpert is teaching. Multicultural specialists should insist that the same standards used to select instructors and to teach content in the other academic fields are used when making curricular and instructional decisions about multicultural content and courses.

The Pragmatic Justification

Second, the pragmatic justification: Advocates of the integration-only model argue that by placing a multicultural specialist on a teaching team, multicultural content can be effectively integrated into the general course.

This form of course integration can cause problems for the students as well as for the multicultural specialist on the team. Multicultural concepts, paradigms, and ideologies are *oppositional* to the paradigms, concepts, and theories taught in most mainstream general methods and curriculum courses. When multicultural concepts and paradigms conflict with the other concepts and paradigms in the general course, students often become angry and confused. The lone multiculturalist on the teaching team often becomes the victim of student hostility and confusion.

Multicultural education asks students to examine some of their latent and unexamined attitudes, beliefs, feelings, and assumptions about U.S. society and culture. Students often find this process a difficult and painful one. Because of the power of context, this introspection and self-analysis becomes even more painful and unsettling when it is experienced in the context of an integrated course in which most of the other content and concepts reinforce the students' mainstream values, concepts, attitudes, and beliefs.

Mainstream Versus Transformative Knowledge

Most of the knowledge in teacher education courses is *mainstream academic knowledge* (Banks, 1993e), which consists of the concepts, principles, theories, and explanations that constitute traditional and established knowledge in the behavioral and social sciences. An important tenet in mainstream academic knowledge is that it is a set of objective truths that can be verified through rigorous and objective research and are uninformed by human interests, values, and perspectives.

In reality, mainstream academic knowledge, while appearing neutral and objective, often presents propositions, concepts, and findings that reinforce dominant-group hegemony and perpetuate racism, sexism, and classism. Influential examples of such mainstream knowledge are the concept of cultural deprivation that emerged in the 1960s (Riessman, 1962), Arthur Jensen's (1969) theory of Black and White intelligence, and the concepts of "at-risk" youth and the "underclass" that are popular today. These concepts are heavily value-laden, yet they masquerade as neutral and objective.

Multicultural education, as conceptualized by the major theorists in the field, is a form of transformative academic knowledge, which consists of paradigms, themes, and explanations that challenge mainstream academic knowledge and that expand the historical and literary canon (Banks, 1993a). Transformative scholars, unlike mainstream scholars, assume that knowledge is not neutral but is heavily influenced by human interests; that all knowledge reflects the social, economic, and political relationships within society; and that an important purpose of transformative knowledge is to help citizens improve society.

During the late 1960s and 1970s, transformative scholars challenged some of the dominant paradigms that were heavily influencing the education of low-income students and students of color (S. S. Baratz & Baratz, 1970), including cultural deprivation theories and theories about how mother-tongue languages adversely affected the learning of standard English.

Transformative scholars interrogate the assumptions, ideological positions, and political interests of the knower (Code, 1991; Collins, 1990; Harding, 1991). Lorraine Code (1991), in her seminal book, *What Can She Know? Feminist Theory and the Construction of Knowledge*, raises this question: "Is the gender of the knower epistemologically significant?" After a rigorous philosophical analysis of this question, she concludes that gender does have a complex influence on the knowledge produced by the knower. Sandra Harding (1991) and Patricia Hill Collins (1990) have reached similar conclusions about the relationship between gender and the knower. Nearly two decades before the work of Code, Collins, and Harding, Joyce Ladner (1973) explored a similar question regarding the influence of race on knowledge in *The Death of White Sociology*. Ladner and her colleagues documented the effects of race on knowing in sociology. Ladner was about two decades ahead of her time; consequently, her message was often criticized rather than praised.

The Political Justification

Finally, the integration-only model must be resisted because the power of the multicultural specialist to control the content and pedagogy of the integrated course is decentered and may completely disappear. Typically, the multicultural specialist is a lone member of a teacher education teaching team and is likely to have an ideology and conception of knowledge highly inconsistent with the other members of the team. The multiculturalist on such teams can easily became marginalized as the "Other." Thus the power relationships within the larger society and within the wider university community are likely to be reproduced on the teaching them.

The MCE + integration model allows the multicultural specialist to control an important course and to serve as a resource person for instructors of other courses who wish to integrate their courses with multicultural concepts, paradigms, and pedagogy in a meaningful way. Many of these instructors need and want staff development in multicultural education. An important and appropriate role for the multicultural specialist is to take the lead in implementing a staff development effort within the school or college of education. Outside consultants and resources are usually required to implement such an effort. Local multicultural specialists can facilitate but can almost never conduct training within their own department, college, or school.

THE FUTURE

The ultimate fate of multicultural education as a discipline will to a large extent be determined by the kind of vision we develop and implement in the field. I believe that its fate will be more akin to anthropology and sociology than to progressive education and intergroup education. However, we must act now to set and pursue a rigorous scholarly and research agenda, develop a cadre of strong academic leaders who will shepherd the field in the future, develop standards for practice in the field, strive to improve classroom practice, and take vigorous steps to assure that multicultural education courses and programs are consistent with a transformative tradition that promotes justice, equality, and human dignity.

II

CULTURAL DEMOCRACY AND CITIZENSHIP EDUCATION

The American dream is a complex and cogent idea that millions of individuals have come to the United States seeking—and that pulls to America each year thousands of immigrants who hope to realize it. This fact is especially significant because the material aspects of the American dream are becoming increasingly elusive for most Americans.

Since the early years of the Republic, individuals from almost every culture, nationality, and ethnic group have been able to become American citizens by declaring allegiance to the American democratic ideology (Gleason, 1980). However, the price for full citizenship was cultural assimilation into the Anglo-Saxon-dominated American national culture. Even when they accepted the American political ideology and became culturally assimilated, groups from continents such as Asia and Africa were unable to enjoy the full benefits of American citizenship because of their physical characteristics. Although the United States became one of the most equitable nations in the world during the early years of the Republic, particular *ideological, cultural,* and *physical* characteristics became prerequisites for a full American identification and for total participation in the body politic.

Ideological requisites for full American citizenship are essential, as they are for civic participation in any democratic nation-state. Each nation-state must have an overarching set of ideals to which all of its citizens have attachments and commitments. In the United States, these ideals include liberty, equality, justice, and human dignity. Each democratic nation-state must also have cultural components that all its citizens must acquire in order to participate fully in the body politic. The skills to speak and write the national language and to make a decent living are needed to be an effective citizen. In the United States, for example, all citizens need to be literate in standard English in order to fully participate in the civic life of the nation.

CULTURAL DEMOCRACY

Cultural democracy, an ideology that emerged in the United States at the turn of the century, was exhumed during the ethnic revitalization movements of the 1960s and 1970s. Philosophers and writers in the early 1900s—such as Horace Kallen, Randolph Bourne, and Julius Draschler, of immigrant background themselves—were strongly committed to cultural freedom for the flood of southern, central, and eastern Europeans who were settling in the United States (Bourne, 1916; Draschler, 1920; Kallen, 1924). They formulated the concepts of *cultural democracy* and *cultural pluralism* to provide a philosophical justification for cultural freedom for the European Americans. When the ethnic revitalization movements of the 1960s and 1970s emerged, groups such as African Americans, Mexican Americans, and American Indians revived these concepts to justify their quests for cultural, economic, and political equity.

A central tenet of cultural democracy is that individuals and groups must have cultural freedom in a democratic nation-state, just as they have political freedom. Political democracy, this position maintains, gives individuals and groups the right to practice their ethnic and community cultures and behaviors as long as they do not conflict with the overarching values and goals of the commonwealth.

Cultural democracy theorists believe that all Americans should internalize American democratic ideals and the elements of the national culture needed to fully participate in the body politic. However, they believe that individuals can internalize American political ideals and become competent in the civic culture while maintaining important aspects of their ethnic and community cultures. Public institutions such as schools, cultural democracy theorists maintain, have the responsibility to help people acquire the skills needed to fully participate in the commonwealth but not the right to alienate them from their primordial cultures. They believe that individuals and groups have both the ability and the right to be bicultural and multicultural in a pluralistic democracy.

CITIZENSHIP EDUCATION AND MULTIPLE IDENTIFICATIONS

Children are socialized in regional, ethnic, social-class, and religious communities in which they develop values, behaviors, and commitments that differ from those of youths socialized in other American communities and microcultures. In addition to developing identifications to their ethnic communities and cultures, students are citizens of the American commonwealth and

acquire national characteristics and attachments. They also live in a world society and are influenced by international events and developments. However,
like other nationals, Americans tend to have weak identifications with the
global community.

Citizenship education should help students to acquire the knowledge,
skills, and values needed to make reflective public decisions consistent with
American political ideals. The effective citizen in a democratic nation-state
has a commitment to the overarching and shared idealized national values
and the skills and commitment to act on them. To help students become
effective citizens of the American commonwealth, the school must help them
to develop clarified, reflective, and positive identifications and attachments
to their *cultural communities*, the *nation-state*, and the *global world society* (Banks, 1988b). Students who have negative and confused identifications
with their local cultures are not likely to develop reflective national attachments. Individuals must have clarified and reflective national identifications
in order to become effective citizens of the global community. Cultural, national, and global identifications are integrally related; each is a requisite to
the other.

Cultural Identification

While there are many definitions of *culture*, we may define it as the unique
values, symbols, life-styles, institutions, and other human-made components
that distinguish one group from another. In the United States, we can describe
the American national culture (the macroculture) as well as the diverse sub-
cultural groups that are integral parts of the American national culture (the
microcultures). We can, for example, distinguish the national culture of the
United States from those of Japan, Nigeria, and India, each of which has a
unique set of characteristics. In *The Chrysanthemum and the Sword: Patterns of Japanese Culture*, Ruth Benedict (1946) discusses some of the modal
characteristics of Japanese culture—such as the importance of loyalty, honor,
shame, and respect for authority—and contrasts them to American culture.

The national character studies written by American anthropologists during the 1940s and 1950s were attempts to describe the macroculture of the
United States using both anthropological and psychological concepts. Anthropologists such as Margaret Mead and Ruth Benedict wrote some of the most
influential examples of this genre. Mead's (1942) book, *And Keep Your Powder Dry*, became one of the best-known of the national character studies. Erik
Erikson's *Childhood and Society* (1950) includes an important chapter on
the American character, "Reflections on the American Identity."

The American national culture, as well as the microcultural groups that
constitute it, can also be described. Examples of microcultural studies include

Ruth Benedict's *Patterns of Culture* (1934), in which she contrasts the Pueblo Indian culture of New Mexico with other North American Indian groups; Shirley Anchor's (1978) ethnography of a Chicano community, *Mexican Americans in a Dallas Barrio*; Jules Henry's (1965) *Pathways to Madness*, a study of five mainstream American suburban families; Elena Padilla's (1958) *Up from Puerto Rico*, a study of New York's Spanish Harlem; and *On the Street Where I Live* by Melvin D. Williams (1981), an ethnography of a Black Pittsburgh neighborhood.

American youths are members of many different cultural groups and have multiple group attachments and identifications. An American child may be simultaneously a Baptist, a southerner, a Girl Scout, a female, an Anglo-Saxon, and an Appalachian. The importance of each of these groups to her at any one time will vary depending on many factors, including the times, the situations in which she finds herself, and her stages of psychological and social development.

Each of the group identifications of students is important and merits careful study by social scientists and educators. However, in this chapter I am using the term *cultural identification* to refer only to those attachments and identifications that relate to regional, religious, social-class, ethnic, and racial groups, groups that are primarily ascriptive and involuntary. I am not using *culture* in this context to describe national character or national culture. In this chapter, *national identification* is used to describe an individual's attachment to his or her nation-state or national culture and *global identification* is used to describe an individual's attachment to the world community.

I am defining *identification* as "a social-psychological process involving assimilating the values, standards, expectations, or social roles of another person or persons . . . into one's behavior and self-conception" (Theodorson & Theodorson, 1969, pp. 194–195). When an individual develops an identification with a particular group, he or she "internalizes the interests, standards, and role expectations of the group" (p. 195). Identification is an evolving, dynamic, complex, and ongoing process, not a static or unidimensional concept. All individuals belong to many different groups and consequently develop multiple group identifications and loyalties.

I am concerned in this chapter with how variables such as race, ethnicity, social class, region, and religion—separately and together—influence the socialization of American youths and result in their having behaviors, speech patterns, values, and worldviews that differ and sometimes conflict with those of other American youths and with mainstream American institutions. The cultural groups that are the focus in this chapter are primarily ascriptive and involuntary, strongly influence the socialization and values of their members, and are primarily groups to which individuals are likely to have deep psychological attachments and primordial affiliations and which evoke a sense of peoplehood and historic attachment. These groups evoke feelings and allegiances of a "we-they" and an "us-them" variety. The attachments that individuals are likely to have to their primordial cultural groups, such as their small neighborhood and their ethnic or religious group, are primarily emotional, nonreflective, unexamined, and unconscious.

The primordial communities in which students are socialized deeply influence their behavior, their notions of what is right and wrong, and their fundamental beliefs about the world in which they live. Students' ideas about the sacred and the secular, and the importance of each in their lives, are also shaped by their cultural communities. Many of the problems that develop between the school and the community, and many of the cultural disparities that students experience, are caused by conflicting values, beliefs, and behavior that are taught by the home and the school. The American school, because of its role and function, has become increasingly secular and scientific since the turn of the century and highly suspicious of and hostile to folk beliefs and cultures. Yet many students are socialized in homes and communities in which the sacred is valued more than the secular and the scientific, and in which traditional cultural beliefs and values are strongly held.

CULTURAL, NATIONAL, AND GLOBAL IDENTIFICATIONS: EDUCATIONAL IMPLICATIONS

We need to determine the most appropriate educational responses to the different and often conflicting behaviors, values, beliefs, and identifications that students bring to school. Our role is certainly not merely to reinforce them. Such an education would be far too limiting and culturally encapsulating. It is also not sufficient to help students attain the values, skills, and abilities needed to fully participate in the national civic culture. Some writers have argued that the school merely reinforces the values and behaviors of mainstream American youths and rarely helps them to better understand other American microcultures or to develop cross-cultural competencies.

While the school should not merely reinforce the parochial cultures of students, it should, however, try to avoid teaching students contempt for their primordial cultures and making them ashamed of their behavior, values, and worldviews. In their eagerness to teach scientific views of the world, teachers often make students feel ashamed for holding sacred beliefs that defy scientific logic. Educators should have as one of their major aims teaching students the scientific, secular, and universal culture of the nation-state, but they should also realize that science and technology, despite their importance in modern life, cannot satisfy all of the important social and psychological needs of humans. Apter (1977) writes: "[Modernization] leaves what might be called a *primordial space*, a space people try to fill when they believe they have lost something fundamental and try to recreate it" (p. 75; emphasis added).

The school curriculum should reflect the reality that students must function both in their private cultures and in the public civic community. It should help students to function in these two worlds by playing a mediating role. It should help students to resolve the conflicts that arise from their functioning in the private world of the home and the neighborhood and in the public world of the school and the nation-state. G. Grant (1981) believes that students are increasingly deserting public for private school because their parents want them educated in a cultural community that has moral authority. The public school should unabashedly promote values that are consistent with the American Creed. It should also respect, but not necessarily promote, the values and behavior that students bring to the classroom and help them to understand how their cultures influence their behavior, values, and worldviews.

It is essential for the school to help students function both in their private neighborhoods and in the civic community and society. However, this ambitious task is fraught with difficulties and uncertainties. There are inherent conflicts between modernity and tradition, and between folk cultures and the culture of the scientific and secular community. However, trying to help students to function effectively in their private and public worlds is an important, if difficult, role for contemporary schools.

Understanding Diverse Cultures

Educators need to develop a sophisticated understanding of the diverse groups to which students belong and to learn how their cultures influence their learning and behavior. Teachers should also help students develop an understanding of their own cultural groups and acquire cultural identifications that are reflective and clarified. Through the process of developing reflective and clarified cultural identifications, students will hopefully acquire more positive attitudes toward their neighborhoods and communities.

Helping students to develop reflective, clarified, and positive identifications with their cultural groups does not mean that we should teach cultural hero worship, group ethnocentrism, and cultural myths and fantasies. Too much of traditional American history teaching commits these sins. Many ethnic studies and women's studies lessons during the 1960s and 1970s also engaged a great deal in myth-making and chauvinism. Teaching should help students to develop clarified and reflective cultural group attachments, to demystify their own cultural groups, to develop an awareness of them as separate cultural entities, and to understand their relationships with other cultural groups both within and outside this nation. Teaching should also help students to understand how their cultural groups influence their behavior and how they shaped the development of American civilization. If these goals are attained, students will be able to objectively view both the functional and dysfunctional characteristics of their cultural groups.

Cultural Influences on Learning

Students from diverse regional, social-class, religious, ethnic, and racial groups often achieve at different levels in the common schools. Students from some groups tend to score better on standardized achievement tests and to experience more success than students who belong to other groups. For example, urban students in the Northwest tend to score better on standardized tests than rural students in the South; Mexican American youths have much higher school dropout rates then mainstream American youths.

A number of researchers are beginning to document how cultural differences can help explain some of the differential achievement scores across social-class, ethnic, and cultural groups. Research by Cole and Bruner (1972), Stodolsky and Lesser (1967), and Ramírez and Castañeda (1974) indicates that culture influences learning, sometime significantly. Other researchers, such as J. C. Baratz and Shuy (1969) and Lambert (1975), have studied how the family languages of students place them at a disadvantage when they must learn concepts in the public language of the school rather than in the languages of their cultural communities.

Helping Students to Develop Self-Understanding

Most students come to school with little consciousness of how their cultures and life-styles are unique and different from those of other American cultural groups. Because most American students attend school in largely homogeneous communities, they often complete their common school experience without having any meaningful first-hand experiences with people from different social-class, religious, racial, or ethnic groups. This is especially likely to be the case for middle-class and upper-class mainstream American students. However, many poor, urban youths also have few opportunities to interact with individuals from other groups. Thus most American youths remain largely culturally encapsulated throughout their experiences in the nation's schools.

An important goal of the school should be to help students develop keen insights into their own cultural groups and to better understand how those groups are both alike and different from other American microcultures. One of the best ways to help students to better understand their own cultures is to help them to view their cultures through the lenses of other cultures. For example, mainstream American youths can better understand their own cultural values and behaviors if they are juxtaposed with those of Jewish and Japanese Americans; African American and Jewish youths can also gain keen insights into their cultures by viewing them from the perspectives of others. By viewing their own through the lenses of other cultures, students will not only develop keener insights into the uniqueness of their own cultures but will also better understand the similarities that characterize all human communities.

National Identification

As important as it is for the school to reflect cultural democracy and to respect and understand the students' cultures, it is also vitally important for all American youths to develop a reflective and clarified national identification and a strong commitment to American political ideals. An important role of the school is to help socialize youths so that they develop the attitudes, values, and competencies needed to fully participate in the nation's civic life.

To maintain a vigorous and healthy democracy, a nation must have a set of overarching, idealized values to which all groups of its citizens must be committed. Myrdal (1944) described the overarching idealized values of our commonwealth as the American Creed, which includes equality, justice, liberty, and human dignity as core values. As in every nation-state, there is a significant gap between our idealized national values and our societal practices. A major goal of each generation should be to help close the gap between our ideals and realities.

When the Republic was founded in 1776, the American dream of equality and justice was limited primarily to White males with property. Yet because of the cogency of the American Creed, various groups have used its tenets to justify their structural inclusion into the social, economic, and political life of the nation. African Americans, women, people with disabilities, and various other groups have attained increasingly more equity through the years by political action for which the American Creed served as a basic tenet.

In his classic study, *An American Dilemma*, Myrdal (1944) argues that the treatment of Blacks in the United States and the existence of the American Creed create an American dilemma in the consciences of most Americans. Myrdal predicted that this American dilemma contained the seeds that would lead to the eradication of blatant segregation and racism in the South and to more racial equality.

The emergence of the civil rights movement of the 1950s and 1960s and the crumbling of legalized segregation in the South supported Myrdal's hypothesis. However, his thesis is controversial in part because race relations remain a significant problem in the United States despite the real and symbolic gains of the 1960s. However, I believe, with Myrdal, that the American Creed is a cogent force in U.S. society and that powerful ideals open up the possibility for social change that can increase equity and human rights.

Despite the power of Myrdal's thesis and his keen predictive insights, he does not adequately consider the other factors that, along with national ideals, motivate humans. Ideals do not influence the behavior of individuals in a vacuum; they interact with an individual's self-interest and other motives. Overarching national ideals, such as those that constitute the American Creed, may win out in some situations, but they can and do lose out in others. In most situations, self-interests conflict with the idealized values and goals of the commonwealth.

Yet the American dream still lives and is a cogent force in American life. Immigrants risk their lives almost daily to reach American shores so that they might share its legendary richness and political ideals. Since 1970, large numbers of immigrants have come to the United States from such nations as Mexico, China, Korea, Vietnam, the Philippines, and Haiti (U.S. Bureau of the Census, 1991). However, the current economic crisis in our nation is severely challenging the American dream, our democratic ideals, and the national will to cope. If present economic trends continue, the gap between the haves and the have-nots will reach crisis proportions. We will become two nations— one rich and one poor. The pernicious gap between the rich and the poor in many Third World nations makes us painfully aware of how rigid social-class stratification can destroy dreams like those embedded in the American Creed. In his poem "Harlem," Langston Hughes (1951/1994) speaks of a deferred dream and points out that one possible consequence of such a dream is that it may explode.

NATIONAL POLICY AND GOALS

Strengthening attachments to the nation-state and its idealized values, developing clearly articulated national policies, and gaining national consensus will considerably strengthen our nation and enable it to face current and future challenges. The United States is being stymied by factionalized self-interest groups that are making contradictory demands on the commonwealth. No one speaks for the commonwealth. Consequently, it suffers enormously because no constituency is organized to promote the overarching interests of the nation-state.

My observations in Japan helped to convince me that a nation-state, to experience maximum economic growth and the potential to solve its major human problems, must have clearly delineated national policies in areas such as industrial growth, health, and education (Banks, 1982). Japanese institutions usually have clearly specified goals and are operated with tremendous efficiency. Because of this, Japan has attained phenomenal economic, educational, and industrial growth since World War II. I was impressed by the ways in which Japanese individuals shared and respected institutional goals and worked to achieve them. Japan has been able to develop a high level of consensus about overarching values and goals for the nation-state and to mobilize to attain them. While there are many complex reasons for Japan's success, its ability to attain a significant consensus on national goals is one of the most important.

Because our nation's history and culture are quite different from Japan's, we cannot reach consensus on national goals in the Japanese way. In the United States, diversity and individuality are two of our most salient and cherished characteristics. These characteristics have enriched our lives and continue to do so. Few Americans are willing to sacrifice them. However, our challenge is to attain some kind of delicate balance between the needs of individuals and special-interest groups and the needs of the commonwealth. We have stressed individuality and diversity to the point that there is little national consensus about what should be the goals of governmental, industrial, health, and educational institutions. We need to build a consensus for a set of national goals and policies that are shared by diverse cultural and interest groups.

The Problems with Americanization

Educational attempts to build reflective nationalism and consensus on national goals are likely to be greeted with strong skepticism and even hostility by some groups because of the history of Americanization movements in the United States (Highham, 1972). The development of a strong national American identity is likely to be associated with forced assimilation, Anglo-conformity, the melting pot, and institutionalized racism.

Since the beginning of the Republic, the United States has been unique in that it allowed most immigrants to become American citizens by making a commitment to American political ideals. The mass culture and industrialization in the United States also gave immigrants rich opportunities to experience social and economic mobility, but they often had to abandon their ethnic characteristics in order to participate fully. Most immigrants found the attractiveness of American institutions and economic opportunities irresistible and forsook many, if not most, of their ethnic characteristics.

The ease with which immigrants could become citizens and the strong appeal of Americanization and America's industrialized culture does not tell the full story of ethnicity and Americanization in the United States. The essence of an American identity was and still is the acceptance of American political ideals. Yet the English Americans so strongly influenced and dominated American institutions that cultural as well as physical appearances emerged as requisites for becoming complete American citizens who could participate fully in the nation's institutions.

By the turn of the century, immigrants from Europe could become legal citizens by declaring allegiance to American democratic ideals, but they could become full participants in American life only by becoming culturally assimilated into the English-dominated culture. Most European immigrants chose full participation in the commonwealth over maintaining attachments to their ethnic roots. However, according to European American scholars who led the "new pluralism" movement of the 1960s—such as Michael Novak (1971) and William Greenbaum (1974)—the Americanization process was often painful for European Americans. Greenbaum maintains that American society, including the schools, eradicated the cultures and languages of immigrant groups by using shame and hope. The immigrants, argues Greenbaum, were taught to disrespect their own cultures but were given hope that once they were no longer ethnic they would gain full inclusion into the nation's industrialized society and enjoy all of the benefits of modernization and industrialization.

Despite the pain that Greenbaum and Novak associate with Americanization, European immigrants could become full Americans by swearing allegiance to American democratic ideals and becoming culturally similar to the English Americans. Yet for decades Americans from non-White lands could not become full Americans even when they accepted American democratic ideals and became culturally assimilated. Most members of these groups diligently tried to become full Americans—assimilated and structurally integrated into American society—but this was denied them because of their physical characteristics. It is much more possible today than it was at the beginning of the civil rights movement in the 1950s for members of these groups to become full Americans and to acquire an American identification. However, we still have a great deal of work to do before Americans from all cultural, racial, and ethnic groups will have equal opportunities to enjoy the full benefits of American democracy.

BUILDING NATIONALISM IN
A CULTURALLY PLURALISTIC DEMOCRACY

The United States, like other Western nations, has traditionally tried to create a cohesive, equitable, and modernized nation-state by establishing a secularized, scientific national culture. The liberal utopians who envision this kind of nation-state visualize a just and equitable society in which individuals from all cultural, ethnic, regional, and religious groups are able to fully participate. However, for this kind of equitable, modernized society to emerge and blossom, individuals must be freed of their communal, primordial, and cultural attachments.

Traditionalism, argues the liberal, is inconsistent with modernization and a technological culture. Traditional cultures promote historic prejudices, we–they attitudes, and cultural conflict. They also lead to the Balkanization of the nation-state. Traditionalism and cultural pluralism also stress group rights over the rights of the individual and regard the group rather than the individual as primary. In a modernized, equitable society, individual rights are paramount; group rights are secondary.

Liberals are also critical of traditionalism because, they maintain, it promotes inequality, racial and ethnic awareness, and group favoritism. As long as attachments to cultural and ethnic groups are salient and emphasized, argues the liberal assimilationist, they will serve as the basis for job and educational discrimination as well as other forms of exclusion that are inconsistent with American Creed values. The solution to this problem, argues the liberal modernist, is a common national culture into which all individuals assimilate and public policies that are neutral on questions of race and ethnicity. Government policies should neither support ethnic or primordial issues nor should they discourage them. Pluralism may remain in a modernized national culture, but it must be based on interests that cut across ethnic and primordial groups. Modernized pluralism is based on factors such as social class, education, and other voluntary and achieved affiliations.

The liberal expects traditional cultural ties and behavior in the enlightened, modernized society to die of their own weight. Give all ethnic, racial, religious, and cultural groups equal opportunities to participate in the modernized nation-state, and attachments to primordial cultures will disappear. If thick primordial cultures persist in a modernized society it is because of aberrations in the liberal solution and because inequality still exists. This constitutes a pathological condition. If you give Mexican Americans full opportunities to participate in American society, they will forget about bilingual education, ethnic rituals, and ethnic interests. The controversy over Black English will die when African Americans become full participants in the national culture.

As Apter (1977) perceptively states, the liberal assimilationist conception of the relationship between tradition and modernity is not so much wrong as it is incomplete, flawed, and oversimplified. The ethnic revitalization movements of the 1960s and 1970s and the quest for moral authority among our youths in recent years indicate that the liberal solution to the problem of traditionalism in a modernized society fails to fulfill some of the fundamental psychological, spiritual, and community needs of humans.

Du Bois's (1953) conception of double-consciousness and the push–pull syndrome helps us to better understand the complex relationship of traditionalism and modernity in mass societies. There is little doubt that the strong appeal of America's industrialized society and its tremendous opportunities for economic and social mobility have motivated most American groups to rid themselves of most aspects of their ethnic cultures and to become skeptical and ashamed of folk cultures and traditionalism. There has been and continues to be a tremendous push toward assimilation in the United States because of the strong appeal of social and economic mobility. Nevertheless, the push toward Americanization is counterbalanced by the trenchant pull of primordialism, traditionalism, and the search for moral authority and meaning in life that mass societies often leave unfulfilled. These counterbalancing factors, which pull individuals toward traditional cultures, have been much stronger in American society than is often acknowledged. They experienced a resurgence during the ethnic revitalization movements of the 1960s and 1970s. Prior to the publication of Glazer and Moynihan's landmark book of 1963, *Beyond the Melting Pot*, most American social scientists endorsed some version of the liberal assimilationist position, assuming that cultural attachments, rapidly vanishing in American society, would in time totally disappear. Their disappearance from the nation would be a healthy and positive development. After all, when ethnicity and racial identifications disappeared from American society, equality would be a reality because individuals would be freed from the burden of primordial cultural attachments and ethnic affiliations. However, as Glazer and Moynihan (1963) perceptively point out: "[Ethnicity] is fixed deep in American life generally; the specific pattern of ethnic differentiation, however, in every generation is created by specific events" (p. 291). Fishman (1966), in his landmark book, *Language Loyalty in the United States*, comments on the cogency of Americanization but notes the persistence of cultural attachments in American society:

> Theoretically, the American melting pot should have been more successful, considering the rapid social mobility which it holds out as an explicit reward, the forces of urbanization and industrialization that support it, and the absence of well-defined or deeply-rooted American cultural patterns which might have conflicted with contrasting immigrant cultures. At the same time this lack of a substantive and traditional core culture may also conduce to a partial failure of the melting pot. . . . There are limits to the ability of larger-scale and more modern bonds and principles to solve the longings of mankind. *The primordial and the modern show a capacity to co-exist side by side, to adjust to each other, and to stimulate each other.* (pp. 31, 405; emphasis added)

The liberal assimilationist position suggests that modernity and primordialism are contradictory forces and are inconsistent. Yet, as social scientists such as Apter and Fishman point out, primordialism and traditionalism co-exist in modernized and modernizing societies. They co-exist in part because of what the assimilationist calls "the pathological condition," that is, ethnic groups such as African Americans and Mexican Americans maintain strong attachments to their ethnic groups and culture in part because they have been excluded from full participation in the nation's social, economic, and political institutions. However, many members of these ethnic groups—as well as members of ethnic groups such as Poles, Italians, and Jews—maintain ethnic affiliations and other cultural and regional attachments for more fundamental reasons. It helps them to fulfill some basic psychological and sociological needs that the thin culture of modernization leaves starving and to answer complex questions about moral authority that mass cultures are incapable of helping individuals to resolve. Oliver (1976) discusses the importance of the community in helping individuals to live meaningful lives:

> Ennui and emptiness . . . develop within people's lives, especially the lives of both the affluent and expendable classes as they discover that status, convenience, and material affluence as well as secular intellectual and artistic expression will not satisfy the human longing to search for ultimate meaning. *This ultimate meaning must come from a moral order by community rituals. . . .* [Modern] people should have the option of living not simply in isolated families linked to corporate service agencies . . . , but should have available the possibility of living within real neighborhoods. (pp. 6–7; emphasis added)

Many individuals in highly modernized societies such as the United States also hold onto their primordial attachments because they help to satisfy communal and personal needs. Their shared cultures provide individuals with a sense of community in mass societies, where they run the high risk of experiencing loneliness, anomie, moral confusion, and uncertainty. Cultural group memberships also provide individuals with a foundation for self-definition and senses of belonging, of shared traditions, and interdependence of fate.

Nationalism and Schooling

The United States, like most other nations, has traditionally tried to develop a strong nationalism in individuals by stressing the nation's strengths, highlighting the weaknesses of other nations, teaching about national heroes and myths, and trying to eradicate primordial cultures. A major assumption held by the modernists who dominate American educational policies is that ethnic and primordial cultures are antithetical to the goals of a modernized and industrialized nation.

The assimilationist liberal position that has historically dominated American national policies has been highly successful, in large part because of the push resulting from the appeal of the rapid social and economic mobility in U.S. society. Yet many individuals in U.S. society still have strong attachments to their cultural groups, both because of historic discrimination and because of the personal, moral, spiritual, and psychological needs that modernized cultures leave unfulfilled.

Civic education that reflects cultural democracy has the most potential for helping individuals and groups to develop strong commitments to the overarching ideals of the nation-state and to become full participants in the nation's civic life. An educational policy that reflects cultural democracy should recognize that both traditionalism and modernity co-exist in modernized and modernizing nation-states and that individuals are capable of having multiple identifications. It is not necessary to alienate individuals from their cultures, neighborhoods, and communities in order to help them develop strong national loyalties. In fact, I believe that individuals must have positive, clarified, and reflective commitments and identifications with their cultural groups before they can develop reflective and positive identifications with the national culture. Goodlad (1979) calls this phenomenon "the philosophy of self-transcendence." He writes: "The philosophy of self-transcendence argues that strong feelings of self-worth are prerequisite to and perhaps instrumental in acquiring close identification with others" (p. xv).

When the school fails to respect and/or recognize the cultures of students, it is very difficult for them to feel a part of the national culture taught in the school. Individuals and groups who do not feel part of the national culture are likely to focus on particularistic concerns and issues, not on the issues and problems of the commonwealth. Thus the school, by becoming a culturally democratic community, can help students from diverse cultures develop a commitment to national values and concerns by respecting, acknowledging, and understanding their diverse cultures.

Berger and Neuhaus (1977) argue that the school often alienates students from their cultures and teaches them contempt for those cultures. They maintain that it is important for the school to help empower what they call "mediating structures," such as the family, neighborhood, and community, in order to strengthen the national civic culture. They define mediating structures as those "institutions standing between the individual in his private life and the large institutions of public life" (p. 2). Berger and Neuhaus argue that individuals often find public institutions such as schools alienating. They write:

> For the individual in modern society, life is an ongoing migration between two spheres, public and private. The mega-structures are typically alienating, that is, they are not helpful in providing meaning and identity for individual exis-

tence. . . . One of the most debilitating results of modernization is a feeling of powerlessness in the face of institutions controlled by those whom we do not know and those values we often do not share. (pp. 2, 7)

GLOBAL IDENTIFICATION: PROBLEMS AND PROMISES

Effective citizenship education mandates that we help students to develop the skills, attitudes, and abilities needed to function effectively within the world community. Students are not only citizens of their communities and the nation-state; they are also citizens of a global society (Becker, 1979). However, while most students have conscious identification with their communities and nation-states, often they are only vaguely aware of their status as world citizens. Most U.S. students do not have a comprehensive understanding of the full implications of their world citizenship.

There are many complex reasons why U.S. students often have little awareness or understanding of their status as world citizens and rarely think of themselves as citizens of a world community. This results partly from the fact that the United States, like most other nation-states, focuses on helping students to develop nationalism rather than on helping them to understand their roles as citizens of the world. The teaching of nationalism often results in students learning misconceptions, stereotypes, and myths about other nations and developing negative and confused attitudes toward them.

Students also have limited awareness of their roles as world citizens because of the nature of the world community itself. The institutions that attempt to formulate policies for the international community—or for groups of nations, such as the United Nations, the Organization of African Unity, and the Organization of American States—are usually weak because of their inability to enforce their policies and recommendations, because of the strong nationalism manifested by their members, and because the international community does not have an effectively mobilized and politically efficacious constituency. Strong nationalism makes most international bodies weak and largely symbolic.

Students find it difficult to view themselves as members of an international community not only because it lacks efficacious governmental bodies but also because there are few heroes, myths, symbols, and school rituals that are designed to help students develop an attachment to and identification with the global community. It is difficult for students to develop identifications with a community that does not have heroes and rituals in which they participate and benefits that can be identified, seen, and touched. If we are serious about helping students to develop global attachments and identifications, we need to identify and/or create international heroes and school rituals.

When educators attempt to help students develop more sophisticated international understanding and identification, they often experience complex problems. It is difficult to gain public support for programs in international education because many parents view global education as an attempt to weaken national loyalty and to undercut traditional American values. Many teachers are likely to view global education as an add-on to an already crowded curriculum and to assign it a low priority. Some teachers, like many of their students, have misconceptions and negative attitudes toward other nations and are likely to perpetuate them in the classroom.

Goals for Global Education

When formulating goals and instructional strategies for global education, educators should be cognizant of the societal and pedagogical constraints. However, they should realize that it is vitally important for today's students to develop a sophisticated understanding of their roles in the world community. Students should also understand how life in their communities influences other nations and the cogent influence that international events have on their daily lives. Global education should have as major goals helping students to develop an understanding of the interdependence among nations in the modern world, developing clarified attitudes toward other nations, and developing a reflective identification with the world community. This latter task is likely to be especially difficult because of the highly ambiguous nature of the international community and the tight national boundaries that exist throughout the world.

Balancing Identifications and Schooling

Cultural and national identifications may prevent the development of effective global commitments and the cooperation among nations that is essential to help resolve the world's problems (Banks, 1988b). Nationalism and national attachments in most nations of the world are strong and tenacious. Strong nationalism that is nonreflective will prevent students from developing reflective and positive global identifications. Nonreflective and unexamined cultural attachments may prevent the development of a cohesive nation with clearly delineated national goals and policies. While we need to help students to develop reflective and clarified cultural identifications, they must also be helped to clarify and strengthen their identifications as American citizens—which means that they will internalize American Creed values and develop commitments to act on them.

Students need to develop a delicate balance of cultural, national, and global identifications and attachments. However, educators often try to help students develop strong national identifications by eradicating their primordial cultures and making them ashamed of their families, folk cultures, and folk beliefs. Civic education in a pluralistic democracy should recognize that students must function both in their private worlds and in the civic community. Effective citizenship education must also reflect the fact that tradition and modernity co-exist in industrialized nation-states and that both tradition and modernity help students to satisfy important human needs.

I believe that cultural, national, and global identifications are developmental in nature and that an individual can attain a healthy and reflective national identification only when he or she has acquired a healthy and reflective cultural identification; individuals can develop a reflective and positive global identification only after they have a realistic, reflective, and positive national identification.

Individuals can develop a clarified commitment to and identification with a nation-state and the national culture only when they believe that they are a meaningful part of the nation-state and that it acknowledges, reflects, and values their culture and them as individuals. A nation-state that alienates and does not structurally include all cultural groups within the national culture runs the risk of creating alienation and causing groups to focus on particularistic concerns and issues rather than on the overarching goals and policies of the commonwealth.

REFERENCES

Aboud, F. E. (1987). The development of ethnic self-identification and attitudes. In J. S. Phinney & M. J. Rotheram (Eds.), *Children's ethnic socialization: Pluralism and development* (pp. 32-55). Beverly Hills, CA: Sage.

Aboud, F. E. (1988). *Children and prejudice.* Cambridge, MA: Blackwell.

Acuña, R. (1972). *Occupied America: The Chicano struggle toward liberation.* San Francisco: Canfield.

Agnes, M. (1947). Influences of reading on the racial attitudes of adolescent girls. *Catholic Educational Review, 45,* 415-420.

Alexander, R. J., Craft, M., & Lynch, J. (Eds.). (1984). *Change in teacher education: Context and provision in Great Britain.* New York: Praeger.

Allport, G. W. (1954). *The nature of prejudice.* Cambridge, MA: Addison-Wesley.

An American vision for the 1990s. (1990, March 26). *Fortune,* pp. 14-16.

Anchor, S. (1978). *Mexican Americans in a Dallas barrio.* Tucson: University of Arizona Press.

Anyon, J. (1980). Social class and the hidden curriculum of work. *Journal of Education, 162*(1), 67-92.

Appleby, J. (1992). Recovering America's historic diversity: Beyond exceptionalism. *The Journal of American History, 79*(2), 419-431.

Apter, D. (1977). Political life and cultural pluralism. In M. Tumin & W. Plotch (Eds.), *Pluralism in a democratic society* (pp. 58-91). New York: Praeger.

Aptheker, H. (1943). *American Negro slave revolts.* New York: International Publishers.

Armento, B. J. (1986). Research on teaching social studies. In M. C. Wittrock (Ed.), *Handbook of research on teaching* (pp. 942-951). New York: Macmillan.

Aronson, E., & Bridgeman, D. (1979). Jigsaw groups and the desegrated classroom: In pursuit of common goals. *Personality and Social Psychology Bulletin, 5,* 438-446.

Aronson, E., & Gonzalez, A. (1988). Desegration, jigsaw, and the Mexican-American experience. In P. A. Katz & D. A. Taylor (Eds.), *Eliminating racism: Profiles in controversy* (pp. 301-314). New York: Plenum.

Au, K. H. P. (1980). Participation structures in a reading lesson with Hawaiian children. *Anthropology and Education Quarterly, 11*(2), 91-115.

Backman, M. E. (1972). Patterns of mental abilities: Ethnic, socioeconomic, and sex differences. *American Educational Research Journal, 9,* 1-12.

Baldwin, J. (1985). A talk to teachers. In J. Baldwin, *The price of the ticket: Collected nonfiction 1948-1985* (pp. 325-332). New York: St. Martin's.

Banks, J. A. (1969). A content analysis of the Black American in textbooks. *Social Education, 33*, 954–957, 963.

Banks, J. A., with Clegg, A. A. (1973). *Teaching strategies for the social studies: Inquiry, valuing, and decision-making.* Reading, MA: Addison-Wesley.

Banks, J. A. (1981). *Multiethnic education: Theory and practice.* Boston: Allyn & Bacon.

Banks, J. A. (1982, September). A journey to Japan: Diversity and consensus, *The Social Studies Professional, 65,* 2.

Banks, J. A., with Sebesta, S. L. (1982). *We Americans: Our history and people* (Vol. 2). Boston: Allyn & Bacon.

Banks, J. A. (1984). Values, ethnicity, social science research, and educational policy. In B. Ladner (Ed.), *The humanities in precollegiate education* (Eighty-Third Yearbook of the National Society for the Study of Education, Part II) (pp. 91–111). Chicago: University of Chicago Press.

Banks, J. A. (1986). Multicultural education: Developments, paradigms, and goals. In J. A. Banks & J. Lynch (Eds.), *Multicultural education in Western societies* (pp. 2–28). New York: Praeger.

Banks, J. A. (1987). *Teaching strategies for ethnic studies* (4th ed.). Boston: Allyn & Bacon.

Banks, J. A. (1988a). Ethnicity, class, cognitive, and motivational styles: Research and teaching implications. *The Journal of Negro Education, 57,* 452–466.

Banks, J. A. (1988b). *Multiethnic education: Theory and practice* (2nd ed.). Boston: Allyn & Bacon.

Banks, J. A., with Clegg, A. A. (1990). *Teaching strategies for the social studies: Inquiry, valuing and decision-making* (4th ed.). White Plains, NY: Longman.

Banks, J. A. (1991a). Multicultural education: Its effects on students' racial and gender role attitudes. In J. P. Shaver (Ed.), *Handbook of research on social studies teaching and learning* (pp. 459–469). New York: Macmillan.

Banks, J. A. (1991b). *Teaching strategies for ethnic studies* (5th ed.). Boston: Allyn & Bacon.

Banks, J. A. (1991–1992). Multicultural education: For freedom's sake. *Educational Leadership, 49,* 32–36.

Banks, J. A. (1992). African American scholarship and the evolution of multicultural education. *The Journal of Negro Education, 61,* 273–286.

Banks, J. A. (1993a). The canon debate, knowledge construction, and multicultural education. *Educational Researcher, 22*(5), 4–14.

Banks, J. A. (1993b). Integrating the curriculum with ethnic content: Approaches and guidelines. In J. A. Banks & C. A. M. Banks (Eds.), *Multicultural education: Issues and perspectives* (pp. 3–28). Boston: Allyn & Bacon.

Banks, J. A. (1993c). Multicultural education: Characteristics and goals. In J. A. Banks & C. A. M. Banks (Eds.), *Multicultural education: Issues and perspectives* (2nd ed.) (pp. 3–28). Boston: Allyn & Bacon.

Banks, J. A. (1993d). Multicultural education for young children: Racial and ethnic attitudes and their modification. In B. Spodek (Ed.), *Handbook of research on the education of young children* (pp. 236–250). New York: Macmillan.

Banks, J. A. (1993e). Multicultural education: Historical development, dimensions, and practice. In L. Darling-Hammond (Ed.), *Review of research in education* (Vol. 19) (pp. 3–49). Washington, DC: American Educational Research Association.

Banks, J. A. (1994a). *An introduction to multicultural education.* Boston: Allyn & Bacon.

Banks, J. A. (1994b). *Multiethnic education: Theory and practice* (3rd. ed.). Boston: Allyn & Bacon.

Banks, J. A. (1995a). Multicultural education: Historical development, dimensions, and practice. In J. A. Banks & C. A. M. Banks (Eds.), *Handbook of research on multicultural education* (pp. 3–24). New York: Macmillan.

Banks, J. A. (1995b). Multicultural education: Its effects on students' racial and gender role attitudes. In J. A. Banks & C. A. M. Banks (Eds.), *Handbook of research on multicultural education* (pp. 617–627). New York: Macmillan.

Banks, J. A. (1996a). Measures of assimilation, pluralism, and marginality. In R. L. Jones (Ed.), *Handbook of tests and measurements for Black populations* (Vol. 2, pp. 269–282). Hampton, VA: Cobb & Henry. (Original work written 1984)

Banks, J. A. (Ed.). (1996b). *Multicultural education, transformative knowledge, and action.* New York: Teachers College Press.

Banks, J. A., & Banks, C. A. M. (Eds.). (1989). *Multicultural education: Issues and perspectives.* Boston: Allyn & Bacon.

Banks, J. A., & Banks, C. A. M. (1995a). Equity pedagogy: An essential component of multicultural education. *Theory into Practice, 34*(3), 152–168.

Banks, J. A., & Banks, C. A. M. (Eds.). (1995b). *Handbook of research on multicultural education.* New York: Macmillan.

Baratz, J. C. (1970). Teaching reading in an urban Negro school system. In F. Williams (Ed.), *Language and poverty: Perspectives on a theme* (pp. 11–24). Chicago: Markham.

Baratz, J. C., & Shuy, R. W. (Eds.). (1969). *Teaching Black children to read.* Washington, DC: Center for Applied Linguistics.

Baratz, S. S., & Baratz, J. C. (1970). Early childhood intervention: The social science base of institutional racism. *Harvard Educational Review, 40*(1), 29–50.

Barr, R. D., Barth, J. L., & Shermis, S. S. (1977). *Defining the social studies* (Bulletin 51). Washington, DC: National Council for the Social Studies.

Battle, E. S., & Rotter, J. B. (1963). Children's feelings of personal control as related to social class and ethnic group. *Journal of Personality, 31*, 482–490.

Becker, J. M. (Ed.). (1979). *Schooling for a global age.* New York: McGraw-Hill.

Benedict, R. (1934). *Patterns of culture.* Boston: Houghton Mifflin.

Benedict, R. (1946). *The chrysanthemum and the sword: Patterns of Japanese culture.* New York: Morrow.

Bereiter, C., & Engelmann, S. (1966). *Teaching disadvantaged children in the preschool.* Englewood Cliffs, NJ: Prentice-Hall.

Berger, P. L., & Luckmann, T. (1966). *The social construction of reality: A treatise in the sociology of knowledge construction.* Garden City, NY: Doubleday.

Berger, P. L., & Neuhaus, R. J. (1977). *To empower people: The role of mediating structures in public policy.* Washington, DC: American Enterprise Institute for Public Policy Research.

Bernard, B. (1987). Re-viewing the impact of women's students on sociology. In

C. Farnham (Ed.), *The impact of feminist research in the academy* (pp. 193–216). Bloomington: Indiana University Press.

Best, D. L., Smith, S. C., Graves, D. J., & Williams, J. E. (1975). The modification of racial bias in preschool children. *Journal of Experimental Child Psychology, 20*, 193–205.

Billig, M., & Tajfel, H. (1973). Social categorization and similarity in intergroup behaviour. *Eruopean Journal of Social Psychology, 3*, 27–52.

Billingsley, A. (1968). *Black families in White America*. Englewood Cliffs, NJ: Prentice-Hall.

Blackwell, J. E. (1985). *The Black community: Unity and diversity* (2nd ed.). New York: Harper & Row.

Blassingame, J. W. (1972). *The slave community: Plantation life in the antebellum South*. New York: Oxford University Press.

Bloom, B. S., Davis, A., & Hess, R. (1965). *Compensatory education for cultural deprivation*. New York: Holt.

Bogatz, G. A., & Ball, S. (1971). *The second year of Sesame Street: A continuing evaluation*. Princeton, NJ: Educational Testing Service.

Bourne, R. S. (1916). Trans-national America. *The Atlantic Monthly, 118.*

Boykin, A. W. (1982). Task variability and the performance of Black and White school children: Vervistic explorations. *Journal of Black Studies, 12*, 469–485.

Bragaw, D. H. (1986). Scope and sequence: Alternatives for social studies. *Social Education, 50*, 484–485.

Branch, T. (1988). *Parting the waters: America in the King years 1954–63*. New York: Simon & Schuster.

Brookover, W., Beady, C., Flood, P., Schweitzer, J., & Wisenbaker, J. (1979). *School social systems and student achievement: Schools can make a difference*. New York: Praeger.

Brooks, J. G., & Brooks, M. G. (1993). *In search of understanding: The case for constructivist classrooms*. Arlington, VA: Association for Supervision and Curriculum Development.

Brown, R. (1995). *Prejudice: Its social psychology*. Cambridge, MA: Blackwell.

Brown v. Board of Education of Topeka. (1954). In *The annals of America* (Vol. 17, pp. 253–258), Chicago: Encyclopedia Britannica, 1968.

Bruner, J. S. (1960). *The process of education*. New York: Vintage.

Buchler, J. (Ed.). (1955). *Philosophical writings of Peirce*. New York: Dover.

Bulmer, M. (1984). *The Chicago school of sociology: Institutionalization, diversity, and the rise of sociological research*. Chicago: University of Chicago Press.

Burnes, K. (1970). Patterns of wisc scores for children of two socioeconomic classes and races. *Child Development, 41*, 493–499.

California State Department of Education. (1987). *History-social science framework for California Public Schools, kindergarten through grade twelve*. Sacramento: Department of Education.

Caplan, A. L. (Ed.). (1978). *The sociobiology debate: Readings on the ethnic and scientific issues concerning sociobiology*. New York: Harper & Row.

Cherryholmes, C. H. (1982). Discourse and criticism in the social studies classroom. *Theory and Research in Social Education, 9*, 57–73.

Clark, K. B. (1965). *Dark ghetto: Dilemmas of social power*. New York: Harper & Row.

Clark, K. B. (1973). Social policy, power, and social science research. *Harvard Educational Review, 43*(2), 113-121.

Clark, K. B., & Clark, M. P. (1939). The development of consciousness of self and the emergence of racial identification in Negro preschool children. *Journal of Social Psychology, 10*, 591-599.

Clark, K. B., & Clark, M. P. (1940). Skin color as a factor in racial identification and preference in Negro children. *Journal of Negro Education, 19*, 341-358.

Code, L. (1991). *What can she know? Feminist theory and the construction of knowledge*. Ithaca, NY: Cornell University Press.

Cohen E. G. (1972). Interracial interaction disability. *Human Relations, 25*, 9-24.

Cohen, E. G. (1986). *Designing groupwork: Strategies for the heterogeneous classroom*. New York: Teachers College Press.

Cohen, E. G. (1994). *Designing groupwork: Strategies for the heterogeneous classroom* (2nd ed.). New York: Teachers College Press.

Cohen, E. G., & Lotan, R. A. (1995). Producing equal-status interactions in the heterogeneous classroom. *American Educational Research Journal, 32*(1), 99-120.

Cohen, E. G., & Roper, S. S. (1972). Modification of interracial interaction disability: An application of status characteristic theory. *American Sociological Review, 37*, 643-657.

Cohen, R. A. (1969). Conceptual styles, cultural conflict, and nonverbal tests of intelligence. *American Anthropologist, 71*, 828-856.

Cole, M., & Bruner, J. S. (1972). Preliminaries to a theory of cultural differences. In I. J. Gordon (Ed.), *Early childhood education* (Seventy-First Yearbook of the National Society for the Study of Education) (pp. 161-179). Chicago: University of Chicago Press.

Coleman, J. S., Campbell, E. Q., Hobson, C. J., McParland, J., Mood, A. M., Weinfeld, F. D., & York, R. L. (1966). *Equality of educational opportunity*. Washington, DC: U.S. Government Printing Office.

Coleman, J. S., Kelly, S. D., & Moore, J. A. (1975, April). *Recent trends in school integration*. Paper delivered at the Annual Meeting of the American Educational Research Association, Washington, DC.

Collins, P. H. (1990). *Black feminist thought: Feminist theory and the construction of knowledge*. New York: Routledge.

Comer, J. P. (1980). *School power: Implications of an intervention project*. New York: Free Press.

Comer, J. P. (1988). Educating poor minority children. *Scientific American, 259*(5), 42-48.

Cook, L., & Cook, E. (1954). *Intergroup education*. New York: McGraw-Hill.

Cortés, C. E., with Metcalf, F., & Hawke, S. (1976). *Understanding you and them: Tips for teaching about ethnicity*. Boulder, CO: Social Science Education Consortium.

Coser, L. A. (1977). *Masters of sociological thought* (2d ed.). New York: Harcourt Brace Jovanovich.

Council of the Great City Schools. (1994). *National urban education goals: 1992-1993 indicators report*. Washington, DC: Author.

Cox, B. G., & Ramírez, M. (1981). Cognitive styles: Implications for multiethnic education. In J. A. Banks (Ed.), *Education in the 80s: Multiethnic education* (pp. 61–71). Washington, DC: National Education Association.

Cross, W. E., Jr. (1991). *Shades of Black: Diversity in African American identity.* Philadelphia: Temple University Press.

Cuban, L. (1989). The "at-risk" label and the problem of urban school reform. *Phi Delta Kappan, 70*(10), 780–801.

Cuban, L. (1991). History of teaching in social studies. In J. P. Shaver (Ed.), *Handbook of research on social studies teaching and learning* (pp. 197–209). New York: Macmillan.

Deloria, V., Jr. (1969). *Custer died for your sins.* New York: Avon.

Delpit, L. (1995). *Other people's children: Cultural conflict in the classroom.* New York: New Press.

Derman-Sparks, L., & the A.B.C. Task Force. (1989). *Anti-bias curriculum: Tools for empowering young children.* Washington, DC: National Association for the Education of Young Children.

DeVries, D. L., Edwards, K. J., & Slavin, R. E. (1978). Biracial learning teams and race relations in the classroom: Four field experiments on teams-games-tournament. *Journal of Educational Psychology, 70,* 356–362.

Dewey, J. (1938). *Experience and education.* New York: Macmillan.

Dow, P. B. (1969). Man: A course of study: An experimental social science course for elementary students. *Man: A course of study talks to teachers.* Cambridge, MA: Education Development Center.

Draschler, J. (1920). *Democracy and assimiliation.* New York: Macmillan.

D'Souza, D. (1991). *Illiberal education: The politics of race and sex on campus.* New York: Free Press.

D'Souza, D. (1995). *The end of racism: Principles for a multicultural society.* New York: Free Press.

Du Bois, W. E. B. (1953). *The souls of Black folk: Essays and sketches.* New York: Blue Heron Press.

Du Bois, W. E. B. (1962). *Black reconstruction in America 1860–1880.* New York: Atheneum. (Original work published 1935)

Du Bois, W. E. B. (1975). *The Philadelphia Negro: A social study.* Millwood, NY: Kraus-Thomson Organization Limited. (Original work published 1899)

Edmonds, R. (1986). Characteristics of effective schools. In U. Neisser (Ed.), *The school achievement of minority children: New perspectives* (pp. 93–104). Hillsdale, NJ: Erlbaum.

Edwards, C. D., & Williams, J. E. (1970). Generalization between evaluative words associated with racial figures in preschool children. *Journal of Experimental Research in Personality, 4,* 144–155.

Elam, S. M. (1972). Editor's introduction to William Shockley. Dysgenics, genetically, raceology: A challenge to the intellectual responsibility of educators. *Phi Delta Kappan, 53*(5), 297.

Elkins, S. M. (1959). *Slavery: A problem in American institutional and intellectual life.* Chicago: University of Chicago Press.

Erikson, E. H. (1950). *Childhood and society*. New York: Norton.

Feagin, J. R., & Sikes, M. P. (1994). *Living with racism: The Black middle-class experience*. Boston: Beacon.

Fishman, J. A., (1966). *Language loyalty in the United States*. The Hague: Mouton and Company.

Franklin, J. H. (1943). *The free Negro in North Carolina, 1790-1860*. New York: Russell & Russell.

Franklin, J. H. (1947). *From slavery to freedom: A history of Negro Americans*. New York: Knopf.

Franklin, J. H. (1976). *Racial equality in America*. Chicago: University of Chicago Press.

Franklin, J. H. (1985). *George Washington Williams: A biography*. Chicago: University of Chicago Press.

Franklin, J. H. (1989). The moral legacy of the Founding Fathers. In J. H. Franklin, *Race and history: Selected essays 1938-1988* (pp. 153-162). Baton Rouge: Louisiana State University Press.

Franklin, J. H. (1993). *The color line: Legacy for the twenty-first century*. Columbia: University of Missouri Press.

Franklin, J. H. (1995). Race and the Constitution in the nineteenth century. In J. H. Franklin & G. R. McNeil (Eds.), *African Americans and the living Constitution* (pp. 21-32). Washington, DC: Smithsonian Institution Press.

Frederick Douglass discusses the fourth of July, 1852. (1968). In H. Aptheker (Ed.), *A documentary history of the Negro people in the United States: From colonial times through the Civil War* (Vol. 1) (pp. 330-334). New York: Citadel Press.

Gage, N. L. (1972). I.Q. heritability, race differences, and educational research. *Phi Delta Kappan, 53*(5), 308-312.

Gardner, H. (1983). *Frames of mind: The theory of multiple intelligence*. New York: Basic Books.

Garner, C. W., & Cole, E. G. (1986). The achievement of students in low-SES settings: An investigation of the relationship between locus of control and field dependence. *Urban Education, 21*, 189-206.

Gay, G. (1981). Interactions in culturally pluralistic classrooms. In J. A. Banks (Ed.), *Education in the 80s: Multiethnic education* (pp. 42-53). Washington, DC: National Education Association.

Gay, G. (1986). Multicultural teacher education. In J. A. Banks & J. Lynch (Eds.), *Multicultural education in Western societies* (pp. 154-177). London: Holt, Rinehart & Winston.

Gay, G. (1993). Ethnic minorities and educational equality. In J. A. Banks & C. A. M. Banks (Eds.), *Multicultural education: Issues and perspectives* (pp. 171-194). Boston: Allyn & Bacon.

Gay, G. (1995). Curriculum theory and multicultural education. In J. A. Banks & C. A. M. Banks (Eds.), *Handbook of research on multicultural education* (pp. 25-43). New York: Macmillan.

Genovese, E. D. (1972). *Roll, Jordan, roll: The world the slaves made*. New York: Pantheon.

Gilligan, C., Lyons, N. P., & Hanmer, T. J. (Eds.). (1990). *Making connections: The relational words of adolescent girls at Emma Willard School.* Cambridge, MA: Harvard University Press.

Glazer, N., & Moynihan, D. P. (1963). *Beyond the melting pot.* Cambridge, MA: MIT Press.

Gleason, P. (1980). American identity and Americanization. In S. Thernstrom, A. Orlov, & O. Handlin (Eds.), *Encyclopedia of American ethnic groups* (pp. 31–58). Cambridge, MA: Harvard University Press.

Goodlad, J. I. (1979). Foreword. In J. M. Becker (Ed.), *Schooling for a global age.* New York: McGraw-Hill.

Gordon, M. (1964). *Assimilation in American life.* New York: Oxford University Press.

Gould, S. J. (1981). *The mismeasure of man.* New York: Norton.

Gould, S. J. (1994). Curveball. *The New Yorker, 70*(38), 139–149.

Grambs, J. D. (1968). *Intergroup education: Methods and materials.* Englewood Cliffs, NJ: Prentice-Hall.

Grant, C. A., & Sleeter, C. E. (1986). Race, class, and gender in education research: An argument for integrative analysis. *Review of Educational Research, 56,* 195–211.

Grant, G. (1981). The character of education and the education of character. *Daedalus, 110,* 135–149.

Greenbaum, W. (1974). America in search of a new ideal: An essay on the rise of pluralism. *Harvard Educational Review, 44,* 411–440.

Gutman, H. G. (1970). *The Black family in slavery and freedom, 1750–1925.* New York: Vintage.

Habermas, J. (1968). *Knowledge and human interests.* Boston: Beacon.

Hale, J. (1981). Black children: Their roots, culture and learning styles. *Young Children, 36,* 37–50.

Hale-Benson, J. (1986). *Black children: Their roots, culture, and learning styles* (rev. ed.). Baltimore: John Hopkins University Press.

Haley, A. (1977). *Alex Haley tells the story of his search for his roots* (Record). Burbank, CA: Warner Brothers Records.

Hanna, P. R. (1963). Revising the social studies: What is needed. *Social Education, 27,* 190–196.

Harding, S. (1991). *Whose science? Whose knowledge? Thinking from women's lives.* Ithaca, NY: Cornell University Press.

Heath, S. B. (1983). *Ways with words: Language, life, and work in communities and classrooms.* New York: Cambridge University Press.

Henry, J. (1965). *Pathways to madness.* New York: Random House.

Herrnstein, R. J. (1971). I. Q. *Atlantic Monthly, 228,* 43–64.

Herrnstein, R. J. (1973). *"I. Q." in the meritocracy.* Boston: Little, Brown.

Herrnstein, R. J., & Murray, C. (1994). *The bell curve: Intelligence and class structure in American life.* New York: Free Press.

Highham, J. (1972). *Strangers in the land: Patterns of American nativism 1860–1925.* New York: Atheneum.

Hilliard, A. (1976). *Alternatives to IQ testing: An approach to the identification of gifted minority children*. Final report to the California State Department of Education, Sacramento.

Hirsch, E. D., Jr. (1987). *Cultural literacy: What every American needs to know*. New York: Houghton Mifflin.

Hirsch, E. D., Jr., Kett, J. F., & Trefil, J. (1988). *The dictionary of cultural literacy: What every American needs to know*. Boston: Houghton Mifflin.

Hohn, R. L. (1973). Perceptual training and its effect on racial preference of kindergarten children. *Psychological Reports, 32*, 435-441.

Hughes, L. (1994). Harlem. In A. Rampersad & D. Roessel (Eds.), *The collected poems of Langston Hughes* (p. 426). New York: Knopf. (Original work published 1951)

Hyatt, V. L., & Nettleford, R. (Eds.) (1995). *Race, discourse, and the origin of the Americas: A new world view*. Washington, DC: Smithsonian Institution Press.

Irvine, J. J., & York, E. D. (1995). Learning styles and culturally diverse students: A literature review. In J. A. Banks & C. A. M. Banks (Eds.), *Handbook of research on multicultural education* (pp. 484-497). New York: Macmillan.

Jackson, E. P. (1944). Effects of reading upon the attitudes toward the Negro race. *The Library Quarterly, 14*, 47-54.

Jackson, P. W. (1992). *Untaught lessons*. New York: Teachers College Press.

Jacoby, R., & Glauberman, N. (Eds.) (1995). *The bell curve debate: History, documents, opinions*. New York: Times Books/Random House.

Jencks, C., Smith, M., Acland, H., Bane, M. J., Cohen, D., Gintis, H., Heyns, B., & Michelson, S. (1972). *Inequality: A reassessment of the effects of family and schooling in America*. New York: Basic Books.

Jensen, A. R. (1969). How much can we boost IQ and scholastic achievement? *Harvard Educational Review, 39*, 1-123.

Johnson, D. W., & Johnson, R. T. (1981). Effects of cooperative and individualistic learning experiences on interethnic interaction. *Journal of Educational Psychology, 73*, 444-449.

Johnson, D. W., & Johnson, R. T. (1991). *Learning together and alone* (3rd ed.). Englewood Cliffs, NJ: Prentice-Hall.

Johnston, W. B., & Packer, A. B. (1987). *Workforce 2000: Work and workers for the 21st century*. Washington, DC: U.S. Government Printing Office.

Kagan, J. A., McViker Hunt, J., Crow, J. F., Bereiter, C., Elkin, D., & Cronbach, L. (1969). Discussion: How much can we boost IQ and scholastic achievement? *Harvard Educational Review, 39*(2), 274-347.

Kallen, H. M. (1924). *Cultural democracy in the United States: Studies in the group psychology of the American people*. New York: Boni & Liveright.

Kamii, C. K., & Radin, N. J. (1967). Class differences in socialization practices of Negro mothers. *Journal of Marriage and the Family, 29*, 302-310; reprinted (1971) in R. Staples (Ed.), *The Black family: Essays and studies* (pp. 235-247). Belmont, CA: Wadsworth.

Katz, M. B. (1989). *The undeserving poor: From the war on poverty to the war on welfare*. New York: Pantheon.

Katz, P. A. (1973). Perception of racial cues in preschool children: A new look. *Developmental Psychology, 8*, 295-299.

Katz, P. A. (1976). Attitude change in children: Can the twig be straightened? In P. A. Katz (Ed.), *Towards the elimination of racism* (pp. 213-241). New York: Pergamon.

Katz, P. A. (1982). A review of recent research in children's attitude acquisition. In L. Katz (Ed.), *Current topics in early childhood education* (Vol. 4) (pp. 17-54). Norwood, NJ: Ablex.

Katz, P. A., Sohn, M., & Zalk, S. (1975). Perceptual concomitants of racial attitudes in urban grade-school children. *Developmental Psychology, 11*, 135-144.

Katz, P. A., & Zalk, S. R. (1978). Modification of children's racial attitudes. *Developmental Psychology, 14*, 447-461.

Kendall, F. E. (1983). *Diversity in the classroom: A multicultural approach to the education of young children.* New York: Teachers College Press.

King, J. E. (1992). Diaspora literacy and consciousness in the struggle against miseducation in the Black community. *The Journal of Negro Education, 61*(3), 317-340.

Kirp, D. L. (1977). School desegregation and the limits of legalism. *Public Interest, 47*, 101-128.

Kleinfeld, J. (1975). Effective teachers of Eskimo and Indian students. *School Review, 83*, 301-344.

Kleinfeld, J., & Nelson, P. (1991). Adapting instruction to Native Americans' learning style: An iconoclastic view. *Journal of Cross-Cultural Psychology, 22*, 273-282.

Kuhn, T. S. (1970). *The structure of scientific revolutions* (2d ed., enl.). Chicago: University of Chicago Press.

Kymlica, W. (1995). *Multicultural citizenship.* New York: Oxford University Press.

Ladner, J. A. (Ed.). (1973). *The death of White sociology.* New York: Vintage.

Ladson-Billings, G. (1990). Like lightning in a bottle: Attempting to capture the pedagogical excellence of successful teachers of Black students. *Qualitative Studies in Education, 3*(4), 335-344.

Ladson-Billings, G. (1994). *The dreamkeepers: Successful teachers of African American children.* San Francisco: Jossey-Bass.

Ladson-Billings, G. (1995a). Multicultural teacher education: Research, practice, and policy. In J. A. Banks & C. A. M. Banks (Eds.), *Handbook of research on multicultural education* (pp. 747-759). New York: Macmillan.

Ladson-Billings, G. (1995b). Toward a theory of culturally relevant pedagogy. *American Educational Research Journal, 32*(3), 465-491.

Lambert, W. E. (1975). Culture and language as factors in learning and education. In A. Wolfgang (Ed.), *Education of immigrant students* (pp. 55-83). Toronto: Ontario Institute for Studies in Education.

Lasker, B. (1929). *Race attitudes in children.* New York: Holt, Rinehart & Winston.

Leacock, B. (1969). *Teaching and learning in city schools.* New York: Basic Books.

Lee, C., & Slaughter-Defoe, D. T. (1995). Historical and socio-cultural influences on African American education. In J. A. Banks & C. A. M. Banks (Eds.), *Handbook of research on multicultural education* (pp. 348-371). New York: Macmillan.

Leftcourt, H. M. (1982). *Locus of control: Current trends in theory and research* (2nd ed.). Hillsdale, NJ: Erlbaum.

Lesser, G. S., Fifer, G., & Clark, D. H. (1965). Mental abilities of children from different social class and cultural groups. *Monographs of the Society for Research in Child Development, 30*(4).

Lewis, B. A. (1991). *The kid's guide to social action*. Edited by P. Espeland. Minneapolis: Free Spirit Publishing.

Lightfoot, S. L. (1988). *Balm in Gilead: Journey of a healer*. Reading, MA: Addison-Wesley.

Litcher, J. H., & Johnson, D. W. (1969). Changes in attitudes toward Negroes of White elementary school students after use of multiethnic readers. *Journal of Educational Psychology, 60*, 148–152.

Litcher, J. H., Johnson, D. W., & Ryan, F. L. (1973). Use of pictures of multiethnic interaction to change attitudes of White elementary school students toward Blacks. *Psychological Reports, 33*, 367–372.

Mannheim, K. (1949). *Ideology and utopia: An introduction to the sociology of knowledge*. New York: Harcourt Brace Jovanovich.

Marker, G., & Mehlinger, H. (1992). Social studies. In P. W. Jackson (Ed.), *Handbook of research on curriculum* (pp. 830–851). New York: Macmillan.

Martin, E. P., & Martin, J. M. (1978). *The Black extended family*. Chicago: University of Chicago Press.

McAdoo, H. P., & McAdoo, J. L. (Eds.). (1985). *Black children: Social, education, and parental environments*. Beverly Hills: Sage.

McIntosh, P. (1990). *Interactive phrases of curricular and personal re-vision with regard to race*. Wellesley, MA: Wellesley College, Center for Research on Women.

Mead, M. (1942). *And keep your powder dry: An anthropologist looks at America*. New York: Morrow.

Mercer, J. R. (1989). Alternative paradigms for assessment in a pluralistic society. In J. A. Banks & C. A. M. Banks (Eds.), *Multicultural education: Issues and perspectives* (pp. 289–304). Boston: Allyn & Bacon.

Merton, R. K. (1968). *Social theory and social structure* (enl. ed.). New York: Free Press.

Metcalf, L. W. (1971). (Ed.). *Values education: Rationale, strategies, and procedures*. Washington, DC: National Council for the Social Studies.

Milner, D. (1983). *Children & race*. Beverly Hills, CA: Sage.

Moore, E. G. J. (1985). Ethnicity as a variable in child development. In M. G. Spencer, G. K. Brookins, & W. R. Allen (Eds.), *The social and affective development of Black children* (pp. 101–115). Hillsdale, NJ: Erlbaum.

Moore, J. W., & Pachon, H. (1976). *Mexican Americans* (2nd ed.). Englewood Cliffs, NJ: Prentice-Hall.

Moynihan, D. P. (1965). *The Negro family: The case for national action*. Washington, DC: U.S. Department of Labor, Office of Planning and Research.

Murray, C. (1984). *Losing ground: American social policy 1950–1980*. New York: Basic Books.

Myrdal, D. (with R. Sternal & A. Rose). (1944). *An American dilemma: The Negro problem in modern democracy*. New York: Harper.

Napierkowski, T. (1976). Stepchild of America: Growing up Polish. In M. Novak (Ed.), *Growing up Slavic in America* (pp. 9-20). New York: Empac.

National Council for the Social Studies. (1979). Revision of the NCSS social studies curriculum guidelines. *Social Education, 43*, 261-278.

New York State Department of Education. (1989). *A curriculum for inclusion* (Report of the Commissioner's Task Force on Minorities: Equity and Excellence). Albany: State Department of Education.

New York State Department of Education. (1991). *One nation, many peoples: A declaration of cultural interdependence* (Report of the New York State Social Studies Review and Development Committee). Albany: State Department of Education.

Newmann, F. M., with Oliver, D. W. (1970). *Clarifying public controversy: An approach to teaching social studies*. Boston: Little, Brown.

Newmann, F. M. (1975). *Education for citizen action: Challenge for secondary curriculum*. Berkeley, CA: McCutchan.

Nieto, S. (1994). Lesson from students on creating a chance to dream. *Harvard Educational Review, 64*(4), 392-415.

Nieto, S. (1995). A history of the education of Puerto Rican students in U.S. mainland schools: "Losers," "outsiders," or "leaders?" In J. A. Banks & C. A. M. Banks (Eds.), *Handbook of research on multicultural education* (pp. 388-411). New York: Macmillan.

Novak, M. (1971). *The rise of the unmeltable ethnics*. New York: Macmillan.

Oakes, J. (1985). *Keeping track: How schools structure inequality*. New Haven, CT: Yale University Press.

Okhiro, G. (1994). *Margins and mainstreams: Asians in American history and culture*. Seattle: University of Washington Press.

Oliver, D. W. (1976). *Education and community: A radical critique of innovative schooling*. Berkeley, CA: McCutchan.

Oliver, D. W., & Shaver, J. P. (1966). *Teaching public issues in the high school*. Boston: Houghton Mifflin.

Olsen, F. (1974). *On the trail of the Arawaks*. Norman: University of Oklahoma Press.

Omi, M., & Winant, H. (1986). *Racial formation in the United States*. New York: Routledge.

Orasanu, J., Lee, C., & Scribner, S. (1979). The development of category organization and free recall: Ethnic and economic group comparisons. *Child Development, 50*, 1100-1109.

Padilla, E. (1958). *Up from Puerto Rico*. New York: Columbia University Press.

Pallas, A. M., Natriello, G., & McDill, E. L. (1989). The changing nature of the disadvantaged population: Current dimensions and future trends. *Educational Researcher, 18*(5), 16-22.

Parish, T. S., & Fleetwood, R. S. (1975). Amount of conditioning and subsequent change in racial attitudes of children. *Perceptual and Motor Skills, 40*, 79-86.

Parish, T. S., Shirazi, A., & Lambert, F. (1976). Conditioning away prejudicial attitudes in children. *Perceptual and Motor Skills, 43*, 907-912.

Parker, W. C. (Ed.). (1996). *Educating the democratic mind*. Albany: State University of New York Press.

Patterson, O. (1977). *Ethnic chauvinism: The reactionary impulse*. New York: Stein & Day.

Pawlowska, H. (1976). The education of Harriet Pawlowska. In M. Novak (Ed.), *Growing up Slavic in America* (pp. 21–27). New York: Empac.

Perney, V. H. (1976). Effects of race and sex on field dependence–independence in children. *Perceptual and Motor Skills, 42*, 975–980.

Perspectives on inequality. (1973). *Harvard Educational Review* (Reprint Series no. 8). Cambridge, MA.

Peters, W. (1987). *A class divided: Then and now* (exp. ed.). New Haven, CT: Yale University Press.

Pettigrew, T. F. (1964). *A profile of the Negro American*. Princeton, NJ: Van Nostrand.

Pettigrew, T. F., & Green, R. L. (1976). School desegregation in large cities: A critique of the Coleman "White flight" thesis. *Harvard Educational Review, 46*(2), 1–53.

Phillips, U. B. (1918). *American Negro slavery*. New York: Appleton.

Phinney, J. S., & Rotheram, M. J. (Eds.). (1987). *Children's ethnic socialization: Pluralism and development*. Beverly Hills, CA: Sage.

Pinkney, A. (1984). *The myth of Black progress*. New York: Cambridge University Press.

Polakow-Suransky, S., & Ulaby, N. (1990). Students take action to combat racism. *Phi Delta Kappan, 71*(8), 601–606.

Popkewitz, T. S. (1977). The latent values of the discipline-centered curriculum. *Theory and Research in Social Education, 5*, 41–60.

Popkewitz, T. S. (1984). *Paradigm and ideology in educational research: The social foundations of the intellectual*. London: Falmer.

Poverty rate is up sharply for very young, study says. (1990, April 16). *The New York Times*, p. A7.

Quarles, B. (1953). *The Negro in the Civil War*. Boston: Little, Brown.

Ramírez, M. (1973). Cognitive styles and cultural democracy in education of Mexican Americans. *Social Science Quarterly, 53*, 895–904.

Ramírez, M., & Castañeda, A. (1974). *Cultural democracy, bicognitive development and education*. New York: Academic.

Ramírez, M., & Price-Williams, D. R. (1974). Cognitive styles of children of three ethnic groups in the United States. *Journal of Cross Cultural Psychology, 5*, 212–219.

Ramsey, P. G. (1987). *Teaching and learning in a diverse world: Multicultural education for young children*. New York: Teachers College Press.

Ravitch, D. (1978). The "White fight" controversy. *Public Interest, 51*(2), 135–149.

Ravitch, D. (1990, Spring). Diversity and democracy: Multicultural education in America. *American Educator*, pp. 16–48.

Ravitch, D., & Finn, C. E., Jr. (1987). *What do our 17-year olds know? A report on the first national assessment of history and literature*. New York: Harper & Row.

Renninger, C. A., & Williams, J. E. (1966). Black–White color connotations and race awareness in children. *Perceptual and Motor Skills, 22*, 771–785.

Richardson, V. (1990). At-risk programs: Evaluation and critical inquiry. In K. A. Sirotnik (Ed.), *Evaluation and social justice: Issues in public education* (pp. 61–75). San Francisco: Jossey-Bass.

Riessman, F. (1962). *The culturally deprived child*. New York: Harper & Row.

Rist, R. C. (1978). *The invisible children*. Cambridge, MA: Harvard University Press.

Rivlin, A. M. (1973). Forensic social science. *Harvard Educational Review, 43*(1), 61–75.

Rothbart, M., & John, O. P. (1993). Intergroup relations and stereotype change: A social-cognitive analysis and some longitudinal findings. In P. M. Sniderman, P. E. Telock, & E. G. Carmines (Eds.), *Prejudice, politics, and the American dilemma* (pp. 32–59). Stanford, CA: Stanford University Press.

Ruse, M. (1979). *Sociobiology: Sense or nonsense?* Boston: Reidel.

Ryan, W. (1971). *Blaming the victim*. New York: Vintage.

Rychlak, J. F. (1975). Affective assessment, intelligence, social class, and racial learning style. *Journal of Personality and Social Psychology, 32*, 989–995.

Sacks, D. O., & Theil, P. A. (1995). *The diversity myth: "Multiculturalism" and the politics of intolerance at Stanford*. Oakland, CA: Independent Institute.

Saracho, O. N., & Spodek, B. (Eds.). (1983). *Understanding the multicultural experience in early childhood education*. Washington, DC: National Association for the Education of Young Children.

Schlesinger, A. M., Jr. (1986). *The cycles of American history*. Boston: Houghton Mifflin.

Schlesinger, A. M., Jr. (1991). *The disuniting of America: Reflections on a multicultural society*. Knoxville, TN: Whittle Direct Books.

Schockley, W. (1972). Dysgenics, geneticity, raceology: A challenge to the intellectual responsibility of educators. *Phi Delta Kappan, 53*(5), 297–307.

School desegregation: The continuing challenge. (1976). *Harvard Educational Review* (Reprint Series no. 11). Cambridge, MA.

Shade, B. J. (1982). Afro-American cognitive style: A variable in school success? *Review of Educational Research, 52*(3), 219–244.

Shade, B. J., & New, C. A. (1993). Cultural influences on learning. In J. A. Banks & C. A. M. Banks (Eds.), *Multicultural education: Issues and perspectives* (2nd ed.) (pp. 317–331). Boston: Allyn & Bacon.

Shaver, J. P. (Ed.). (1977). *Building rationales for citizenship education* (Bulletin 52). Washington, DC: National Council for the Social Studies.

Shaver, J. P. (Ed.). (1991). *Handbook of research on social studies teaching and learning*. New York: Macmillan.

Shaver, J. P., Davis, O. L., Jr., & Helburn, S. W. (1979). The status of social studies education: Impressions from three NSF studies. *Social Education, 43*, 150–153.

Siegel, I., Anderson, L. M., & Shapiro, H. (1966). Categorization behavior in lower- and middle-class preschool children: Differences in dealing with representation of familiar objects. *Journal of Negro Education, 35*, 218–229.

Slavin, R. E. (1979). Effects of biracial learning teams on cross-racial friendships. *Journal of Educational Psychology, 71*, 381–387.

Slavin, R. E. (1983). *Cooperative learning*. New York: Longman.

Slavin, R. E. (1985). Cooperative learning: Applying contact theory in desegregated schools. *Journal of Social Issues, 41*, 45–62.

Sleeter, C. A. (1995). An analysis of the critiques of multicultural education. In J. A.

Banks & C. A. M. Banks (Eds.), *Handbook of research on multicultural educa-tion* (pp. 81-94). New York: Macmillan.

Sleeter, C. E., & Grant, C. A. (1987). An analysis of multicultural education in the United States. *Harvard Educational Review, 57,* 421-444.

Sleeter, C. E., & Grant, C. A. (1991). Race, class, gender, and disability in current textbooks. In W. W. Apple & L. K. Christian-Smith (Eds.), *The politics of the textbook* (pp. 78-101). New York: Routledge.

Smedley, A. (1993). *Race in North America: Origin and evolution of a worldview.* Boulder, CO: Westview Press.

Smitherman, G. (1977). *Talking and testifying: The language of Black America.* Boston: Houghton Mifflin.

Spencer, M. B. (1982). Personal and group identity of Black children: An alternative synthesis. *Genetic Psychology Monographs, 106,* 59-84.

Spencer, M. B., & Horowitz, F. D. (1973). Effects of systematic social and token rein-forcement on the modification of racial and color concept attitudes in Black and in White preschool children. *Developmental Psychology, 9,* 246-254.

Stampp, K. M. (1956). *The peculiar institution: Slavery in the ante-bellum South.* New York: Vintage.

Steinfels, P. (1979). *The neoconservatives: The men who are changing America's politics.* New York: Simon & Schuster.

Stephan, W. G. (1985). Intergroup relations. In G. Lindzey & E. Aronson (Eds.), *The handbook of social psychology* (3rd ed.) (pp. 599-658). New York: Random House.

Stodolsky, S. S., & Lesser, G. (1967). Learning patterns in the disadvantaged. *Harvard Educational Review, 37,* 546-593.

Superka, D. P., Hawke, S., & Morrissett, I. (1980). The current and future status of social studies. *Social Education, 44,* 362-369.

Taba, H. (1967). *Teachers' handbook for elementary social studies.* Palo Alto, CA: Addison-Wesley.

Tajfel, H. (1970). Experiments in intergroup discrimination. *Scientific American, 223*(5), 96-102.

Tetreault, M. K. T. (1993). Classrooms for diversity: Rethinking curriculum and peda-gogy. In J. A. Banks & C. A. M. Banks (Eds.), *Multicultural education: Issues and perspectives* (2nd ed.) (pp. 129-148). Boston: Allyn & Bacon.

Theodorson, G. A., & Theodorson, A. (1969). *A modern dictionary of sociology.* New York: Barnes & Noble.

Thompson, C. H. (1932). Editorial comment: Why a Journal of Negro Education? *The Journal of Negro Education, 1*(1), 1-4.

Thornton, R. (1995). North American Indians and the demography of contact. In V. L. Hyatt & R. Nettleford (Eds.), *Race, discourse, and the origin of the Ameri-cas: A new world view* (pp. 213-230). Washington, DC: Smithsonian Institu-tion Press.

Todorov, T. (1982). *The conquest of America: The question of the other.* New York: HarperCollins.

Trager, H. G., & Yarrow, M. R. (1952). *They learn what they live: Prejudice in young children.* New York: Harper & Brothers.

Trotman, F. K. (1977). Race, IQ, and the middle class. *Journal of Educational Psychology, 69,* 266-273.

Tucker, W. H. (1994). *The science and politics of racial research.* Urbana: University of Illinois Press.

Turner, F. J. (1989). The significance of the frontier in American history. In C. A. Milner II (Ed.), *Major problems in the history of the American West* (pp. 2-21). Lexington, MA: Heath. (Original work published 1894)

Tye, B. B. (1987). The deep structure of schooling. *Phi Delta Kappan, 69*(4), 281-284.

U.S. Bureau of the Census. (1991). *Statistical abstract of the United States: 1991* (111th edition). Washington, DC: U.S. Government Printing Office.

U.S. Bureau of the Census. (1994). *Statistical abstract of the United States: 1994* (114th ed.). Washington, DC: U.S. Government Printing Office.

U.S. Commission on Civil Rights. (1967). *Racial isolation in the public schools.* Washington, DC: U.S. Government Printing Office.

Valencia, S., Hiebert, E. H., & Afflerbach, P. P. (Eds.). (1994). *Authentic reading assessment: Practices and possibilities.* Newark, DE: International Reading Association.

Valentine, C. A. (1968). *Culture and poverty: Critique and counter proposal.* Chicago: University of Chicago Press.

van den Berghe, P. L. (1981). *The ethnic phenomenon.* New York: Elsevier.

Vasquez, J. A. (1979). Bilingual education's needed third dimension. *Educational Leadership, 37,* 166-168.

Vygotsky, L. S. (1978). *Mind in society: The development of higher psychological processes.* Cambridge, MA: Harvard University Press.

Warner, W. L. (1949). *Social class in America.* Chicago: Science Research Associates.

Weiner, M. J., & Wright, F. E. (1973). Effects of undergoing arbitrary discrimination upon subsequent attitudes toward a minority group. *Journal of Applied Social Psychology, 3,* 94-102.

White, J. L. (1984). *The psychology of Blacks.* Englewood Cliffs, NJ: Prentice-Hall.

Williams, J. E., & Edwards, C. D. (1969). An exploratory study of the modification of color and racial concept attitudes in preschool children. *Child Development, 40,* 737-750.

Williams, J. E., & Morland, J. K. (1976). *Race, color and the young child.* Chapel Hill: University of North Carolina Press.

Williams, M. D. (1981). *On the street where I live.* New York: Holt.

Williams, R. L. (1971). Abuses and misuses in testing Black children. *Counseling Psychologist, 2*(3), 62-73.

Wilson, E. O. (1978). *Human nature.* Cambridge, MA: Harvard University Press.

Wilson, R., & Melendez, S. E. (1987). *Minorities in higher education.* Washington, DC: American Council on Education.

Wilson, W. J. (1978). *The declining significance of race: Blacks and changing American institutions.* Chicago: University of Chicago Press.

Winant, H. (1994). *Racial conditions: Politics, theory, comparisons.* Minneapolis: University of Minnesota Press.

Witkin, H. A. (1950). Individual differences in ease of perception of embedded figures. *Journal of Personality, 19,* 1-15.

Witkin, H. A. (1962). *Psychological differentiation.* New York: Wiley.

Witkin, H. A., & Goodenough, D. R. (1981). *Cognitive styles: Essence and origins.* New York: International Universities Press.

Woodson, C. G. (1930). *The Negro in our history.* Washington, DC: Associated Publishers.

Woodson, C. G. (1933). *The mis-education of the Negro.* Washington, DC: Associated Publishers.

Woodson, C. G. (1968). *The education of the Negro prior to 1861.* New York: Arno Press. (Original work published 1915)

Yawkey, T. D., & Blackwell, J. (1974). Attitudes of 4-year-old urban Black children toward themselves and Whites based upon multi-ethnic social studies materials and experiences. *The Journal of Educational Research, 67,* 373-377.

INDEX

ABOUT THE AUTHOR

JAMES A. BANKS is Professor and Director of the Center for Multicultural Education at the University of Washington, Seattle. He is president of the American Educational Research Association (AERA) and a past president of the National Council for the Social Studies (NCSS). Professor Banks has written or edited 15 books in multicultural education and in social studies education. His books include *Teaching Strategies for Ethnic Studies*, 6th Edition; *Multiethnic Education: Theory and Practice*, 3rd Edition; *Teaching Strategies for the Social Studies*, 4th Edition; and (with Cherry A. McGee Banks), *Multicultural Education: Issues and Perspectives*, 3rd Edition. Professor Banks has written over 100 articles, contributions to books, and book reviews for professional publications. He is the editor of the *Handbook of Research on Multicultural Education* and of *Multicultural Education, Transformative Knowledge*, and *Action* (Teachers College Press, 1996).

Professor Banks received the AERA Research Review Award in 1994 and the Distinguished Career Contribution Award from the AERA Committee on the Role and Status of Minorities in Educational Research and Development in 1996.